## STEPHEN MULRINE

Stephen Mulrine is a Glasgow-born poet and playwright. He has written extensively for radio and television, and published many translations. In addition to five plays by Chekhov, published by Nick Hern Books, his translations from Russian range from Pushkin, Gogol, Turgenev and Gorky, to contemporary works by Gelman, Petrushevskaya and Yerofeev, whose cult 1970s novel *Moscow Stations*, adapted as a monologue in 1994, was performed by Tom Courtenay in Edinburgh, London and New York. Other translations published by Nick Hern Books include several plays by Ibsen, and works by Molière, Marivaux and Beaumarchais. English Touring Theatre have premiered a number of Stephen Mulrine's Ibsen and Chekhov versions, and his *Uncle Vanya* was selected in 2008 to open the Rose Theatre, Kingston-upon-Thames, by Sir Peter Hall, who also commissioned his translations of Ibsen's *A Doll's House* and Chekhov's *Swansong* for the Theatre Royal Bath.

# CHEKHOV: SHORTS

THE BEAR

THE PROPOSAL

A TRAGIC FIGURE

THE WEDDING

SWANSONG

ON THE EVILS OF TOBACCO

*translated and introduced by Stephen Mulrine*

## NICK HERN BOOKS
London
www.nickhernbooks.co.uk

**A Nick Hern Book**

*Chekhov: Shorts* first published in Great Britain as a paperback original in 2014 by Nick Hern Books Limited, The Glasshouse, 49a Goldhawk Road, London W12 8QP

This collection of plays copyright in the translation from the Russian © 2014 Stephen Mulrine

Copyright in the introduction © 2014 Nick Hern Books Ltd

Stephen Mulrine has asserted his moral right to be identified as the translator of this work

Designed and typeset by Nick Hern Books Ltd
Printed in the UK by Mimeo Ltd, St Ives, Cambs, PE27 3LE

A CIP catalogue record for this book is available from the British Library

ISBN 978 1 84842 291 9

**CAUTION** All rights whatsoever in these plays are strictly reserved. Requests to reproduce the text in whole or in part should be addressed to the publisher.

**Amateur Performing Rights** Applications for performance, including readings and excerpts, by amateurs in the English language throughout the world (including stock performances in the United States and Canada) should be addressed to the Performing Rights Manager, Nick Hern Books, The Glasshouse, 49a Goldhawk Road, London W12 8QP, *tel* +44 (0)20 8749 4953, *e-mail* info@nickhernbooks.co.uk, except as follows:

*Australia:* Dominie Drama, 8 Cross Street, Brookvale 2100, *fax* (2) 9938 8695, *e-mail* drama@dominie.com.au

*New Zealand:* Play Bureau, PO Box 9013, St Clair, Dunedin 9047, *tel* (3) 455 9959, *e-mail* play.bureau.nz@xtra.co.nz

*South Africa:* DALRO (pty) Ltd, PO Box 31627, 2017 Braamfontein, *tel* (11) 712 8000, *fax* (11) 403 9094, *e-mail* theatricals@dalro.co.za

**Professional Performing Rights** Applications for performance by professionals in any medium and in any language throughout the world (except for stock performances in the United States and Canada) should be addressed to Alan Brodie Representation Ltd, Paddock Suite, The Courtyard, 55 Charterhouse Street, London EC1M 6HA, *fax* +44 (0)20 7183 7999, *web* www.alanbrodie.com

No performance of any kind may be given unless a licence has been obtained. Applications should be made before rehearsals begin. Publication of these plays does not necessarily indicate their availability for performance.

**Contents**

| | |
|---|---|
| Introduction | 7 |
| For Further Reading | 16 |
| Key Dates | 17 |
| Pronunciation Guide | 19 |
| *The Bear* | 21 |
| *The Proposal* | 41 |
| *A Tragic Figure* | 61 |
| *The Wedding* | 71 |
| *Swansong* | 91 |
| *On the Evils of Tobacco* | 103 |

## Introduction

*Anton Chekhov (1860–1904)*

Anton Pavlovich Chekhov was born in Taganrog, a seaport in South Russia, in 1860. By his own account, his childhood was far from idyllic. His father Pavel was a domestic tyrant, fanatically religious, and Chekhov and his brothers were forced to rise before dawn to sing in the local church choir, then work long hours after school in the family grocer's shop.

Taganrog was in decline, but its Greek shipping community was relatively wealthy, and Chekhov was first sent to a Greek-language school, which his father naively regarded as the highway to a lucrative career. After a wasted year, Chekhov was enrolled in the local high school, where he stayed, an unremarkable scholar, until 1879.

His last years at the Taganrog school were spent apart from his family, however, since his bankrupt father had fled to Moscow, where Chekhov's elder brothers were already students. Chekhov completed his studies, entered Moscow University's Faculty of Medicine and, at the age of nineteen, became the family's principal breadwinner, writing short comic pieces to supplement his student allowance.

By the time he qualified in 1884, Chekhov's literary ambitions were already in conflict with what he regarded as his true vocation. Indeed, throughout his life until his own health collapsed, he continued to practise medicine, mostly as an unpaid service to nearby rural communities. Chekhov was almost certainly infected with tuberculosis from childhood, and the disease was in its terminal stages before he would permit an independent diagnosis. In addition to frequent haemorrhaging from the lungs, which forced him to spend the winters in the warm south, Chekhov also suffered from a variety of other chronic ailments, yet his work rate was little short of heroic. In

1899, when he agreed to sell the rights in his works to the publisher Marks, they already filled ten volumes, and the critical consensus is that his short stories are an unparalleled achievement, with the four great plays of his mature dramatic method, *The Seagull*, *Uncle Vanya*, *Three Sisters* and *The Cherry Orchard*, no less important.

Human relationships are the substance of all Chekhov's work, and it is perhaps no surprise that this most intimate of writers remained elusive in his own. Although fond of women, and pursued by several, Chekhov characteristically retreated as they advanced, and it is a reasonable assumption that the happiness of his brief married life, with the actress Olga Knipper, depended to an extent on the lengthy periods of separation forced on the couple by the dramatist's poor health, and Olga's busy metropolitan career.

Finally, in a despairing effort to postpone the inevitable, Chekhov travelled with Olga to Germany for medical treatment. In July 1904, following a heart attack, he died in the spa town of Badenweiler, at the age of forty-four.

*Chekhov's Short Plays: The Vaudevilles*

Chekhov's short plays, mostly written in the late 1880s, while he was establishing his reputation as a short-story writer, are variously subtitled 'monologue', 'farce', 'dramatic scene', etc., but in letters to friends and colleagues they are described as 'vaudevilles' regardless of their content, and generally disparaged as being of no great merit. Certainly, they were written at high speed. *Swansong*, for example, with a running time of some twenty minutes, took him just over an hour to write, and his first attempt at *On the Evils of Tobacco*, in 1886, occupied him a mere two and a half hours. However, to put that in the context of Chekhov's near-superhuman work rate, in one year alone, 1885, he produced over a hundred short stories, so that he might indeed justly claim, as he does in a letter to Suvorin of 23rd December 1888, celebrating the phenomenal success of *The Bear*, that 'subjects keep spouting out of me like oil from the bowels of the earth in Baku'.

Although Chekhov's prose works in total vastly exceed his dramatic output, his earliest serious writing, a full-length play of which only the title, *Fatherlessness*, is known, was completed while he was still in Taganrog, and sent to his brother Alexander in Moscow, along with some comic sketches, also lost. And as soon as the young medical student arrived in the city to rejoin his family in their overcrowded basement flat, he launched a parallel career as a jobbing writer, initially supplying the needs of comic papers like *The Dragonfly* and *The Alarm-Clock*. His early fascination with the drama, however, had never left him, and a fresh attempt at a full-length play, now known as *Platonov*, was offered to the actress Yermolova and rejected, probably in 1881, coming to light in a locked safe only in 1920.

By 1882, Chekhov had achieved the status of featured contributor to the popular St Petersburg weekly *Fragments*, establishing himself on a path which would lead to the award of the Pushkin Prize for literature in 1888, and publication that same year of a short story, *The Steppe*, in a prestige 'thick journal', *The Northern Herald*. In the interim, Chekhov had graduated from Moscow University, received his licence to practise medicine, and moved to more comfortable lodgings.

Broadly speaking, Chekhov's vaudevilles belong to this period of his busy life and were written, it would seem, as a form of relief from more stressful commitments. The great dramatic works of his maturity combine comic and tragic elements with sublime artistry, the balance constantly shifting as they play on our emotions like a subtle and complex piece of music; the vaudevilles, by comparison, are coarser grained and more direct, the comic mechanisms more obvious, and it is interesting in this regard, that Tolstoy, who disliked Chekhov's plays, was fulsome in his praise of the vaudevilles.

With very few exceptions, Chekhov's short plays are self-evidently comic. One notable exception, *On the High Road*, adapted in 1885 from an earlier short story, is perhaps the least 'Chekhovian' of all his works, more suggestive of Gorky's *Lower Depths*, with its melodramatic plot and chance assortment

of misfits thrown together in a roadside tavern. If anything, it
shows Chekhov striving to create 'serious' drama, even as the
flow of comic short stories from his pen was at its peak.
*Swansong*, written the following year, and also adapted from a
short story, is essentially a lachrymose reminiscence by an
ageing actor, who sustains our interest with occasional flashes of
his waning powers, but self-pity so overt as a rule receives short
shrift in Chekhov's work, and is exposed to ridicule, as in *On the
Evils of Tobacco*, a monologue of 1886, in which the henpecked
Nyukhin's 'scientific' lecture metamorphoses into a painfully
funny account of domestic misery.

Chekhov's most popular vaudeville, *The Bear*, was written in
1888 shortly after the completion of his major short story, *The
Steppe*, and in a letter to an acquaintance, Ya. P. Polonsky, he
indeed confesses that he is so exhausted by *The Steppe* that he
can't put his mind to anything serious. *The Bear* was intended
for performance by an actor Chekhov admired, N.N. Solovtsov,
chosen for his impressive physique and deep booming voice,
though Chekhov later came to the opinion that himself and his
sister Masha could have made a better job of it than Solovtsov
and the actress Rybchinskaya did. The memoirist A.S. Lazarev
incidentally records hearing Chekhov himself read *The Bear*
aloud, speaking all the parts and gesticulating with great
animation, despite the fact that he had already by that time
experienced two bouts of pulmonary haemorrhage, in 1884 and
1886, clear evidence of the tuberculosis which would claim his
life in 1904.

*The Bear*, premiered at Korsh's private theatre in Moscow on
28th October 1888, was an instant hit. Unfortunately, a mishap
with a coffee pot cost Chekhov the services of Rybchinskaya,
and the play closed soon after. By March of the following
year, however, it had been staged in Kharkov, Kaluga, Poltava,
Novocherkassk, Taganrog, Revel, Kronstadt, Tomsk, Kiev,
Tula, Tiflis, Kazan, Yaroslavl, Ivanovo-Vozkresensk,
Kostroma and Simbirsk, thoroughly justifying Chekhov's
observation in a letter to his sister, that he ought to have titled
it *The Milch Cow*.

Buoyed up by the success of *The Bear*, Chekhov almost immediately set to work on *The Proposal*, which he described in a letter to I.L. Leontiev in November 1888 as a 'wretched, mangy little thing', good enough for the provinces, but not worth putting on in Moscow or St Petersburg. It was, in fact, premiered at the St Petersburg Artistic Circle on 12th April 1889, and staged at the Alexandrinsky in September of that same year. *The Proposal* is incidentally the only one of Chekhov's plays to be translated into English during the playwright's lifetime, as *A Marriage Proposal*, published by the Athena Society in 1903.

*A Tragic Figure*, subtitled 'A Scene from Dacha Life', is adapted from a short story of 1887, *One of the Many*. In his characteristic self-deprecating manner, Chekhov describes it in a letter to his fellow playwright Leontiev as having a 'hackneyed' theme, and indeed its much put-upon hero, a civil servant left behind in his Moscow office while his relentlessly demanding family enjoy life in their summer cottage, is a stock period type. Leontiev, who had himself written a comedy titled *A Dacha Husband*, believed Chekhov was encroaching on his territory and was sufficiently annoyed to note in his diary: 'Not very comradely of you, Antoine!' *A Tragic Figure* was premiered in the German Club in St Petersburg on 1st October 1889, and at the Abramova Theatre in Moscow a few weeks later.

*The Wedding* derives from a number of sources, chiefly two short stories of 1884, *Marriage for Money* and *A Wedding with a General*, with additional material Chekhov wrote for his brother Nikolai's series of illustrations in 1881, titled *The Wedding Season*. Chekhov's contemporaries also claimed to recognise some of the character originals, including the Greek pastry cook Dymba, modelled on a regular caller at his father's Taganrog grocery shop, while the bride's somewhat affected mother, Zmeyukina, is said to have been based on a guest at a wedding Chekhov attended in Novocherkassk. It's also worth noting that the Chekhov family lived for a time in Moscow directly underneath an apartment which was regularly hired out for wedding parties, with music and dancing into the small hours.

*The Wedding* was accepted by the Maly Theatre and scheduled to open on 15th June 1890. However, that was also the date chosen for the premiere of Shakespeare's *Macbeth*, and Chekhov decided to withdraw his vaudeville on the grounds that: 'With audiences in the mood for Shakespeare's harmony, this play is in danger of appearing rather crude...' *The Wedding* was eventually premiered at the Hunters' Club in Moscow on 28th November 1900, along with *Swansong*, *The Bear*, *The Proposal* and *The Anniversary*, as part of a Chekhov soirée, notably honoured by the presence of Tolstoy, who is said to have laughed uproariously throughout.

Chekhov constantly disparages the vaudevilles in his correspondence, affecting to see them as mere sources of easy money, and a letter of October 1888, offering advice to a budding playwright, A.N. Maslov, fairly summarises his declared stance: 'If you don't have the time to devote to a large-scale work, write some sort of one-acter. I'll have two one-act plays on this season, one with Korsh, the other in a public theatre. I wrote both of them in my spare time. I don't much care for theatre, I soon tire of it, but I do enjoy vaudevilles. I also believe in vaudevilles as an author: the man who can lay claim to a hundred acres, or ten half-decent vaudevilles, is well provided for – his widow will never starve...' Similarly, in a letter of 14th January 1887, addressed to M.V. Kiselyova, Chekhov observes that: 'In general, short plays are much easier to write than long ones; they have very few pretensions and are successful – what more can one ask?'

In truth, Chekhov took great care over his vaudevilles, revising them at every opportunity, and the monologue *On the Evils of Tobacco* is a case in point. A.S. Lazarev recalls criticising Chekhov's decision to include it in his 1885 collection, *Motley Stories*. Chekhov at first seemed to accept the criticism, but then sprang to its defence, as Lazarev observes, 'like a mother especially protective of a sickly child'. Chekhov would go on tinkering with that same monologue, progressively darkening its tone through several recensions, until the last in 1902, when, for long periods, as his condition worsened, he had barely enough energy to put pen to paper. Perhaps Chekhov's true feelings emerged when Stanislavsky, learning that Chekhov had agreed to allow its publication in the periodical *Niva*, wrote to express his dismay at the fact that it would now be possible for Chekhov's publisher Marks to stage it even before the Moscow Art Theatre. Chekhov's response to Stanislavsky was swift: 'Are you out of your mind? The Art Theatre staging a monologue with one character who talks all the time and does nothing?'

*The Vaudevilles Post-Revolution*

In the years after the October Revolution of 1917, Chekhov's status in his homeland markedly declined. The travails of the propertied class and the bourgeoisie in general, as he represents them, were of little interest to the Soviet power, and the poet Mayakovsky expressed a widely held view that the new man of the Revolution wanted something more from theatre than 'Uncle Vanya and Auntie Manya making small talk on the settee.' Productions of Chekhov's work were accordingly rare, but two stagings of the vaudevilles are worth a mention. In the spring of 1921, the avant-garde director Yevgeny Vakhtangov staged *The Wedding* as a grotesque parable in which the guests were portrayed as automata, less than human, and strongly suggesting the doomed revellers at the 'feast in time of plague' of Boccaccio's *Decameron*. Vakhtangov, formerly with the Moscow Art Theatre, had initially rejected Stanislavsky's method in pursuit of what he termed 'fantastic realism', but by the 1920s, satire ruled the roost, with the empty lives of the bourgeoisie and their vulgar ostentation the predictable targets.

Vakhtangov enjoyed a great deal of artistic freedom but died tragically young, of natural causes, in 1922. However, by the time the celebrated Soviet director Vsevolod Meyerhold staged a production of three vaudevilles in 1935, marking the seventy-fifth anniversary of Chekhov's birth, the cultural landscape had changed radically, with the promotion of Socialist Realism as the ruling orthodoxy in all the arts, not least theatre. Meyerhold's homage to Chekhov grouped *The Bear*, *The Proposal* and *The Anniversary* under one title, *33 Swoons*, or *Fainting Fits* – a reference to the total number of these episodes in the three plays. Meyerhold had last directed a Chekhov play in 1904, when he staged *The Cherry Orchard* with his own company a few weeks after its premiere at the Moscow Art Theatre. In artistic terms he shared Vakhtangov's dissatisfaction with the meticulously detailed naturalism which had been the hallmark of the Art Theatre's house style, and also treated Chekhov's farces as vehicles for satire. Meyerhold's theory of 'biomechanics' – emphasising physical activity, the external aspects of performance, often acrobatic, at the expense of psychological relationships – inevitably tended to dehumanise the characters, despite the addition of 'mood' music, by Tchaikovsky, Greig, Strauss, Offenbach and others, to accompany each fainting fit. Meyerhold's production was not well received, however, and it was generally felt that Chekhov's lightweight vaudevilles were unequal to their heavy burden of social comment. More damning, the new orthodoxy of Socialist Realism demanded positive role models, and Meyerhold's 'formalist' approach to theatre soon cost him not only his position, but eventually also his life in February 1940, when he was executed on Stalin's orders.

Chekhov's plays were slow to penetrate the English-speaking world, the first professional production taking place in November 1909, with George Calderon's staging of *The Seagull* at the Royalty Theatre, Glasgow. A production of *The Bear*, in May 1911 at the Kingsway Theatre, London, is chiefly of interest in that it was directed by Lydia Yavorskaya, a celebrated actress and contemporary of Chekhov, with whom she enjoyed a brief, turbulent liaison. Thereafter, the next of the vaudevilles to be professionally produced was *The Proposal*, at the Birmingham Repertory Theatre in March 1916, and the St James Theatre, London, in December 1918. In the intervening year, *The Wedding* was staged at the Grafton Galleries in May 1917. In January 1920, the St Martin's Theatre presented three of Chekhov's one-act plays – *The Bear*, *The Wedding* and *On the High Road*, directed by the pioneer feminist Edith Craig, daughter of the *grande dame* of Victorian theatre, Ellen Terry, and sister of the avant-garde designer Edward Gordon Craig.

While productions of Chekhov's major plays steadily increased in number over the next few decades, the vaudevilles remained something of a rarity, but in February 1949, Laurence Olivier directed Constance Garnett's translation of *The Proposal* at the Old Vic, with Peter Cushing in the role of Lomov. *On the Evils of Tobacco* was presented at the Little Theatre Haymarket in April 1964, under the title *Smoking is Bad for You*, and in June 1967, an opera by William Walton based on *The Bear*, libretto by Paul Dehn, was staged at Aldeburgh. Other notable events include *Swansong*, with Ian McKellen and Edward Petherbridge, the inaugural production at the Sheffield Crucible in November 1971. In February 1978, *The Bear* was staged at the Royal Court Theatre, starring Pauline Collins and David Suchet. The following year, the same play was the inspiration in part for a musical comedy, titled *A Day in Hollywood/A Night in the Ukraine*, which opened at the Mayfair Theatre before transferring to Broadway. And in September 1988, four of the vaudevilles – *Swansong*, *The Bear*, *The Proposal* and *Smoking is Bad for You*, with a cast including Timothy West, Cheryl Campbell and Rowan Atkinson, directed by Ronald Eyre, were presented at the Aldwych.

More recently, in April 2008, BBC Radio 3 rebroadcast *Swansong* as a tribute to the memory of Paul Scofield, who had played Svetlovidov, supported by Alec McCowen as the prompter, in its original 2006 production. And in November 2010, a series of vaudevilles – *The Dangers of Tobacco*, *The Bear*, *The Proposal* and *The Reluctant Tragic Hero*, filmed for television by Baby Cow Productions and starring the comedians Steve Coogan, Johnny Vegas and Julia Davis, was transmitted by Sky Arts.

Finally, in the selection of vaudevilles presented here, *Swansong* was premiered on 14 July 2009 at Bath Theatre Royal, with Peter Bowles in the role of Svetlovidov, and James Laurenson as the Prompter, directed by Sir Peter Hall; and *On the Evils of Tobacco*, commissioned by Shakespeare at the Tobacco Factory, with Paul Brendan as Nyukhin, directed by Andrew Hilton, was premiered in Bristol on 29 March 2012.

## For Further Reading

Among biographies of Chekhov, Ronald Hingley's *A New Life of Chekhov*, Oxford University Press, 1976, is outstanding not only for its wealth of detail, but also the care the author takes to disentangle the man from the work. Also recommended are Ernest J Simmon's *Chekhov: A Biography,* University of Chicago Press, 1962, and Donald Rayfield's *Chekhov: A Life,* HarperCollins, 1997. Maurice Valency's *The Breaking String*, Oxford University Press, 1966, and David Magarshack's *The Real Chekhov*, George Allen & Unwin, 1972, remain perceptive and readable studies of the plays, joined by Richard Gilman's excellent *Chekhov's Plays: An Opening into Eternity,* Yale University Press, 1995.

*Anton Chekhov Rediscovered*, edited by Senderovich and Sendich, Russian Language Journal, 1987, includes a comprehensive bibliography of works in English relating to Chekhov, and *A Chekhov Companion*, edited by Toby W. Clyman, Greenwood Press, 1985, contains useful articles on themes ranging from social conditions in late nineteenth-century Russia, to the critical tradition, both native and Western. Chekhov's reception in the West, over the period 1900–1945, is also documented in detail by Viktor Emeljanow, in *Chekhov, the Critical Heritage*, Routledge & Kegan Paul, 1981. *Chekhov on Theatre,* compiled by Jutta Hercher and Peter Urban, and translated by Stephen Mulrine, Nick Hern Books, 2012, is a collection drawn from Chekhov's journalism and correspondence throughout his working life as dramatist and critic.

Patrick Miles' *Chekhov on the British Stage*, Cambridge University Press, 1993, is a collection of essays by several hands, and contains a chronology of British productions of Chekhov up to 1991. More recently, *The Cambridge Companion to Chekhov,* eds. Vera Gottlieb and Paul Allain, Cambridge University Press, 2000, is an invaluable anthology of essays on a wide range of topics, including the shorter plays. These are also considered at length in the introduction to *Chekhov: 'The Vaudevilles',* translated by Carol Rocamora, and published by Smith and Kraus, Inc., Lyme, New Hampshire, 1998.

## Key Dates

1860  Born 17th January in Taganrog, a port on the Sea of Azov.

1875  Father's grocery business fails, family flees to Moscow, leaving Chekhov behind.

1879  Sets off for Moscow, to enter the Medical Faculty of Moscow University.

1880  First comic story published in *The Dragonfly*, a St Petersburg weekly.

1884  Graduates from university, begins medical practice in Moscow. First symptoms of tuberculosis.

1885  Contributes short stories to the *St Petersburg Gazette*. Writes *On the High Road*.

1886  First short-story collection: *Motley Tales*. Contributes to *New Time*. Writes *On the Evils of Tobacco*.

1887  Second collection: *In the Twilight*. First performance of *Ivanov* at Korsh's Theatre, Moscow, 19th November. Writes *Calchas*, later retitled *Swansong*.

1888  First major story, *The Steppe*, published in the *Northern Herald*. Awarded Pushkin Prize for Literature, by the Imperial Academy of Sciences. Premieres of *The Bear* and *Swansong*. Writes *The Proposal*.

1889  Premieres of *The Proposal* and *A Tragic Figure*. Writes *The Wedding*. First performance of *The Wood Demon* at Abramova's Theatre, Moscow, 27th December.

1890  Travels across Siberia to carry out research on the penal colony of Sakhalin Island.

1891  Writes *The Anniversary*.

1896  Disastrous first performance of *The Seagull*, at the Alexandrinsky Theatre in St Petersburg, 17th October.

1898 Begins association with the Moscow Art Theatre. Worsening tuberculosis forces him to move to Yalta. On 17th December, first successful performance of *The Seagull*, by the Moscow Art Theatre.

1899 First Moscow performance of *Uncle Vanya*, by the same company, 26th October. Publication begins of 'Collected Works', in ten volumes.

1901 First performance of *Three Sisters*, 31st January. Marries the Moscow Art Theatre actress Olga Knipper.

1902 Final revision of *On the Evils of Tobacco*.

1903 Publishes last short story, *The Betrothed*.

1904 First performance of *The Cherry Orchard*, 17th January. Dies in Badenweiler, Germany, 2nd July.

## Pronunciation Guide

Where the stress in English polysyllables tends to fall on the penultimate syllable, Russian stress is less predictable and this gives rise to pronunciation difficulties, quite apart from its unfamiliar consonant clusters. The following is an approximation of those names, etc., which might present difficulty in the spoken text.

*The Bear*
| | |
|---|---|
| Nikolai Mikhailovich | Nee-koh-LAI Mee-KHAI-loh-vitch. |
| Stepan Stepanovich | Styeh-PAN Styeh-PAH-noh-vitch |
| Ryblovo | RIB-loh-va |
| Korchagin | Kawr-CHA-gheen |
| Vlasov | VLAH-soff |
| Grigory Stepanovich | Gree-GOH-ree Styeh-PAH-noh-vitch |
| Smirnov | Smeer-NOHFF |
| Gruzdev | GROOZ-dyehff |
| Yaroshevich | Yah-ROH-sheh-vitch |
| Kuritsyn | Koo-REET-sin |
| Mazutov | Mah-ZOO-toff |
| Semyon | Sehm-YAWN |
| Pelageya | Peh-lah-GAY-ah |

*The Proposal*
| | |
|---|---|
| Ivan Vasilievich | Ee-VAHN Vah-SEEL-yeh-vitch |
| Lomov | LOH-moff |
| Nastasya Mikhailovna | Nah-STAS-ya Mee-KHAI-lohv-na |
| Marusky | Mah-ROO-skee |
| Volchanetsky | Vawl-cha-NYET-skee |

*A Tragic Figure*
| | |
|---|---|
| Ivan Ivanych | Ee-VAHN Ee VAH-nitch |
| Khrapov | KHRAH-pohff |
| Volodya Vlasin | Vaw-LOH-dyah VLAH-seen |
| Vikhrin | VEE-khreen |
| Krivulya Ivanovna | Kree-VOOL-ya Ee-VAH-nohv-na |
| Pavlovna | PAHV-lohv-na |
| Petrushka | Peh-TROOSH-ka |
| Marya | MAHR-ya |

*The Wedding*
| | |
|---|---|
| Andrei Andreyich | Ahn-DREY Ahn-DREY-itch |
| Epaminond Maximych | Eh-pah-mee-NAWND Mahk-SEE-mitch |
| Aplombov | Ah-PLAWM-boff |
| Dashenka | DAH-shehn-ka |
| Martynovna | Mar-TEE-nohv-na |
| Fyodor Yakovlevich | FYAW-dor YAH-kohv-lyeh-vitch |
| Revunov-Karaulov | Reh-voo-NOHFF Kah-rah-OO-lohff |
| Dymba | DEEM-ba |
| Andryusha | Ahn-DRYOO-sha |
| Nastasya Timofeyevna | Nah-STAS-ya Tee-moh-FEY-ehv-na |
| Kharlampy Spiridonych | Khar-LAHM-pee Spee-ree-DOH-nitch |
| Ivan Mikhailych | Ee-VAHN Mee-KHAI-litch |
| Osip Lukich | OH-seep LOO-kitch |
| Babelmandevsky | Bah-bel-mahn-DYEHV-skee |

*Swansong*
| | |
|---|---|
| Yegorka | Yeh-GOR-ka |
| Petrushka | Peh-TROOSH-ka |
| Vassily | Vah-SEE-lee (Vah-SEEL) Vah-SEEL-yitch |
| Boris Godunov | Baw-REES Gah-doo-NOHFF |
| Tsarevich | Tsah-RYEH-vitch |
| Poltava | Pawl-TAH-va |

*On the Evils of Tobacco*
| | |
|---|---|
| Ivan Ivanovich Nyukhin | Ee-VAHN Ee-VAH-no-vitch NYOO-kheen |
| Varvara | Vahr-VAH-ra |
| Natalya Semyonovna | Nah-TAHL-ya Sem-YAW-nohv-na |

# THE BEAR

*A farce in one act*

(*Dedicated to N.N. Solovtsov*)

**Characters**

YELENA IVANOVNA POPOVA, *a young widow with dimples in her cheeks, a landowner*

GRIGORY STEPANOVICH SMIRNOV, *a landowner in his middle years*

LUKA, *Popova's old manservant*

*The action takes place in the drawing room of* POPOVA*'s country house.*

POPOVA, *in deep mourning, her gaze fixed on a small photograph, and* LUKA.

LUKA. It isn't right, ma'am. You're killing yourself. The maid and the cook've gone off berry-picking, glad of a breath of fresh air, even the cat understands that. She's out in the yard chasing sparrows, and here's you stuck in your room the whole day, like in a nunnery, taking no sort of pleasure in life. That's the honest truth, ma'am. That's nigh on a year now, and you haven't once stepped outside the house.

POPOVA. And I never shall! Why should I? My life's already over. He's lying in his grave, and I've buried myself within these four walls. We're both dead.

LUKA. That's plain daft, ma'am. I can't stand to listen to it. Nikolai Mikhailovich is dead, so be it. That's God's will, and may he rest in peace. You've grieved for him, done what's right and proper, but that's enough. You can't mourn him for ever. Same thing happened to me once, when my old woman died. And what then? Well, I grieved for her, cried the best part of a month, I did, but that's as much as she got. I wasn't going to weep and wail the rest of my days, she wasn't worth it. (*Sighs.*) You've shut out all your neighbours, too – never visit, never have them in the house. You'll excuse my saying, ma'am, but we live here like spiders, never see the light of day. And the mice have started eating my livery... Fair enough, if there weren't any company to be had, but there's no shortage of fine gentlemen hereabouts. There's a whole regiment of them over at Ryblovo – officers, a real treat, you'd never weary looking at them. Friday nights, they have a dance there at the barracks, and there's a brass band too, most days. Oh, ma'am, ma'am – you're a good-looking young woman. Peaches and cream, as they say. You should be out there enjoying life. Beauty won't last for ever, you know. In ten years' time, you'll want to be up and doing, giving the officers the glad eye, but it'll be too late.

POPOVA (*firmly*). Please don't ever speak to me on that subject again! As you well know, my life has lost all meaning since my husband died. You may think I'm alive, but it only appears so. I swore to wear these mourning weeds, and shut myself away from the world until my dying day. Do you understand? Let his ghost see how much I love him. Yes, I know, it's no secret – you're well aware of how badly he treated me at times, how cruel he was, and… and unfaithful, even. But I will be true to him to the grave, I'll show him how much I can love. And he'll find me there, beyond the grave, just as I was before he died…

LUKA. You don't want to talk like that, ma'am, truly – you'd be far better going for a stroll round the garden. Or get them to harness up Toby or Giant, look in on the neighbours…

POPOVA. Aahh! (*Begins to weep.*)

LUKA. Ma'am! Ma'am, what's the matter? God Almighty, ma'am!

POPOVA. Oh, he was so fond of Toby! It was always Toby he took, driving over to the Korchagins' place, or the Vlasovs'. And he drove so wonderfully well, he looked so graceful sitting there, pulling on the reins with all his might, d'you remember? Oh, Toby, Toby! Make sure they give him an extra bag of oats today, do.

LUKA. Yes, ma'am. (*A loud ring at the door.*)

POPOVA (*startled*). Who's that? Tell them I'm not in.

LUKA. Yes, ma'am. (*Goes out.*)

POPOVA (*alone, gazing at the photograph*). Now you'll see, *mon cher Nicolas*, how I can love, and forgive… My love will fade away only with myself, when this poor heart of mine stops beating. (*Laughs, through tears.*) Don't you feel guilty? Here I am, your good little faithful wife, I've locked myself away, and I'll be true to you until my dying day, while you… you spoiled brat, have you no conscience? You betrayed me, made terrible scenes, left me alone for weeks on end…

LUKA (*enters, agitated*). There's someone asking for you, ma'am. Wants to see you…

POPOVA. Didn't you tell them I haven't seen anyone since my husband died?

LUKA. I told him, ma'am, but he wouldn't listen – says it's extremely urgent.

POPOVA. I'm not in!

LUKA. That's what I told him, but he's like some sort of devil – just swore at me and barged straight through. He's in the dining room now.

POPOVA (*irritated*). Oh, all right – bring him in. Honestly, that's so rude.

LUKA *goes out*.

People are such a pain. What on earth do they want with me? Why can't they just leave me in peace? (*Sighs*.) I really will have to go into a nunnery… (*Pauses for thought*.) Yes, a nunnery…

SMIRNOV (*entering, to* LUKA). Idiot, you talk too much – silly ass! (*Catches sight of* POPOVA, *adopts dignified manner*.) Madam, allow me to introduce myself: Grigory Stepanovich Smirnov, lieutenant of artillery retired, and landowner. I'm obliged to disturb you on a matter of extreme importance…

POPOVA (*not offering her hand*). What do you want?

SMIRNOV. I had the honour to be acquainted with your late husband, madam, who departed this life in my debt to the tune of twelve hundred roubles – on two separate IOUs. I have to make an interest payment to the bank tomorrow, and I've come to ask you for the money I'm owed – today…

POPOVA. Twelve hundred roubles... What exactly did my husband owe you the money for?

SMIRNOV. He used to buy his oats from me.

POPOVA (*sighs, turns to* LUKA). Yes... Don't forget, Luka – tell them to give Toby his extra bag of oats.

LUKA *goes out*.

(*To* SMIRNOV.) Well, if my late husband owes you something, then of course I'll pay, but I'm afraid I've no money today. My steward will be back from town the day after tomorrow and I'll get him to pay you whatever's owing, but I'm sorry, there's nothing I can do about it at present. What's more, it's seven months to the day since my husband died, and I'm in no mood to discuss money matters.

SMIRNOV. And I'm in no mood to go up in smoke feet first, which is what I'll do if I don't pay that interest tomorrow. They'll set the bailiffs onto me.

POPOVA. You'll get your money, the day after tomorrow.

SMIRNOV. I need it today, not the day after tomorrow.

POPOVA. Well, I'm sorry, I can't give it to you today.

SMIRNOV. I can't wait till the day after tomorrow.

POPOVA. And I can't help it if I've no money today.

SMIRNOV. You mean you can't pay?

POPOVA. That's right – I can't.

SMIRNOV. And that's your last word on the subject?

POPOVA. It is.

SMIRNOV. Your last word? You're positive?

POPOVA. Positive.

SMIRNOV. Well, thank you most humbly. I'll make a note of that, shall I? (*Shrugs*.) And I'm supposed to keep calm? You know, on the way over here I ran into the customs man, and he says to me, 'Grigory Stepanovich,' he says, 'Why are you always in such a foul temper?' Well, I beg your pardon, but I don't see how I can help it. I'm in desperate need of money, I go out yesterday morning at the crack of dawn, chase round all these people who owe me money, and not one of them coughs up! I'm worn out, dog-tired, spend the night in some godawful Jewish tavern, up against the vodka barrel, and then wind up here, fifty miles from home, hoping to get paid, and how am I treated? She's 'not in the mood'! Why wouldn't I be in a foul temper?

POPOVA. I thought I'd made myself clear. You'll get your money when my steward comes back from town.

SMIRNOV. Damn it, it's not your steward I'm after, it's you! What the hell – if you'll excuse me – do I want with your steward?

POPOVA. I beg your pardon, sir, but I'm not accustomed to that sort of language, or to that tone of voice. I won't hear another word... (*Quickly goes out.*)

SMIRNOV (*alone*). Well, how do you like that? She's 'not in the mood'... Her husband died seven months ago, no less! And have I got to pay my interest or haven't I? I'm asking you – have I to pay or not? Oh, but of course, your husband died, you're not in the mood and all that nonsense. Your steward's cleared off, God rot him, and what am I supposed to do? Fly away in a balloon somewhere, to escape my creditors? Take a run at a brick wall and bash my brains in? I go to Gruzdyev's place, he's not in. Yaroshevich is in hiding somewhere. Had a stand-up battle with Kuritsyn, damn near threw him out the window. Mazutov's got the runs, and this one – this one's not in the mood! Not one of the swines'll pay! I've been too damn soft with them, that's the trouble, gone at them like some pathetic dishrag, like some old woman. Been too polite, too nice! Well, just you wait! You'll find out what I'm really like! You're not playing me for a fool, by God you're not! I'm staying right here, I'm not budging, till she pays me. Grrr! I'm so angry today, absolutely spitting mad. Look at me, I'm shaking all over, I

can hardly breathe... Whew! Dear God, I feel quite ill...
(*Shouts.*) Hey, you there!

LUKA (*enters*). Yes, what d'you want?

SMIRNOV. Bring me some beer, or a glass of water!

LUKA *goes out*.

What kind of logic is this? A man's in desperate need of money, he's ready to hang himself, and she won't pay, don't you know, because she's not in the mood to concern herself with money matters! Now how's that for twisted feminine logic? That's why I don't like talking to women, never have done. I'd feel more comfortable sitting on a barrel of gunpowder. (*Shudders.*) Brrr! Sends shivers up my spine, it does. Trailing around in that long frock, she drives me wild. Poetry in motion, hah! The minute I spot one of those creatures on the horizon it sets off a cramp in both legs! That's how mad I get. I feel like shouting for help.

LUKA (*enters, gives* SMIRNOV *a glass of water*). The mistress isn't well. She's not seeing anybody.

SMIRNOV. Oh, get out!

LUKA *goes out*.

Not well, not seeing anybody! So don't, then – go right ahead. I'm staying put, and I'll sit here till you hand over my money. You can be ill for a week, I'll sit here for a week. Make it a year if you like, I'll still be here. I'll get what's owed to me, dear lady! Widow's weeds and dimples in your cheeks won't work on me. We're well up on dimples, yes. (*Shouts out of the window.*) You can unhitch them, Semyon, we're not leaving in a hurry. I'm staying here. Tell the lads in the stable to give the horses some oats... Watch what you're doing, you idiot – you've got that beast tangled up in the reins again! (*Mimics him.*) ''Tain't nuthin'' – I'll give you ''Tain't nuthin''! (*Moves away from the window.*) Sickening! The heat's unbearable, nobody'll give me my money, I've had a rotten night's sleep, and on top of that, this creature swanning around in her widow's weeds and her moods! And now I've a splitting headache. A drop of vodka, maybe? Yes, good idea. (*Shouts.*) Hey, you out there!

LUKA (*enters*). What do you want?

SMIRNOV. Bring me a glass of vodka.

LUKA *goes out.* SMIRNOV *sits down and looks at himself.*

A fine-looking specimen, right enough. Covered in dust, filthy boots, unwashed, uncombed, straw sticking out of my waistcoat. It'd be no surprise if her ladyship took me for a burglar. (*Yawns.*) Not exactly the done thing, turning up in a drawing room in this outfit. Well, what the hell, I'm not a guest, I'm a creditor, and there's no dress code for creditors.

LUKA (*re-enters and hands him a glass of vodka*). You're going a bit over the score, sir...

SMIRNOV (*angrily*). What?

LUKA. I mean... I don't... it's none of my...

SMIRNOV. Who the hell d'you think you're talking to? Just shut up!

LUKA (*aside*). Looks like we're stuck with this devil – must've got blown in on an ill wind! (*Goes out.*)

SMIRNOV. Oh, they've driven me mad! I'm so mad I could pulverise the whole world! It's making me ill... (*Shouts.*) Hey, you out there!

POPOVA (*enters, with downcast eyes*). Good sir, in my solitude I have long been unaccustomed to the sound of a human voice, and I cannot bear shouting. I beg you, most urgently, not to disturb my peace.

SMIRNOV. Pay me my money, and I'll be off.

POPOVA. I've already told you, in plain language, I don't have any spare money today – you'll have to wait till the day after tomorrow.

SMIRNOV. And I've already told you, also in plain language, that I need that money not the day after tomorrow, but today.

And if you don't pay me today, I'll have to hang myself tomorrow.

POPOVA. But how can I help it if I've no money? Oh, this is outrageous!

SMIRNOV. So you're not going to pay me?

POPOVA. I can't...

SMIRNOV. Well, in that case, I'm going to sit right here till I get it. (*Sits down.*) Day after tomorrow, you say? That's just dandy! I'll sit here like this till the day after tomorrow. Like this, see? Just sit... (*Jumps up.*) Look, I'm asking you a question: have I got to pay that interest tomorrow, or haven't I? D'you think I'm joking?

POPOVA. Please don't raise your voice to me, sir – this isn't the stables.

SMIRNOVA. I'm not asking you about the stables. I'm asking you: have I got to pay that interest tomorrow, or not?

POPOVA. Honestly, you have no idea how to behave in the company of a lady.

SMIRNOV. Yes, I have. I know perfectly well how to behave in the company of a lady.

POPOVA. No, you don't. You're an ill-bred, extremely rude man! Decent people don't speak like that to ladies.

SMIRNOV. Oh, this is unbelievable! So how would you like me to address you? In French, is that it? (*Angrily, in an affected simper.*) *Ah, je vous prie, madame* – I am so happy that you are not paying me my money. *Pardon*, that I am troubling you. What beautiful weather we are having today! And how charming *madame* looks in her black dress! (*Bowing and scraping.*)

POPOVA. That's rude, and not very clever.

SMIRNOV (*mimicking her*). Rude, and not clever! Don't know how to behave in female company! Well, let me tell you, madam, I've known more women than you've had hot

dinners! I've fought three duels over women, pistols, no less!
I've dumped twelve women, and nine have dumped me –
yes, indeed! I've made a complete ass of myself in my day,
gone all sickly-sweet and sloppy, grovelled with the best of
them. I've loved, suffered, sighed at the moon, dissolved,
melted, turned to ice. I've loved passionately, insanely, every
way imaginable, damn it, chattered like a demented magpie
about female emancipation, squandered half my fortune on
*feelings*, for God's sake, but not any more, no thank you,
madam, I've had enough! Dark eyes, eyes full of passion,
crimson lips, dimpled cheeks, moonlight, whisperings,
faintness of breath – it's not worth a damn now, dear lady,
none of it! Present company excepted, of course, all women,
from little to large, are prissy, mealy-mouthed
scandalmongers; spiteful, practised liars to the marrow of
their bones; empty-headed, small-minded, merciless logic-
twisters. As far as up here is concerned... (*Taps his
forehead.*) Quite frankly, if you'll forgive my saying, a
common house sparrow could run rings round your petticoat
philosophers. Take any one of these exquisite poetic
creations – light as gossamer, ethereal, a demi-goddess,
she'll transport you to untold ecstasies. Yes, then peer into
her soul – a common-or-garden crocodile! (*Grabs hold of the
back of a chair, which cracks and breaks.*) And worst of all,
what really annoys me, this same crocodile, God knows why,
fancies itself the privileged possessor of a monopoly on
tender feelings, they're its life's work, no less! Damn it to
hell, you can hang me upside-down right here, but since
when did a woman ever love anything but her pet poodle? A
woman in love does nothing but whimper and snivel. Where
a man suffers and makes sacrifices, a woman shows her love
by flapping her petticoats at him, while she sets about
leading him by the nose. You know what women are like,
since you have the misfortune to be one yourself. But just
tell me this, in all honesty – have you ever in your life seen a
genuinely sincere, faithful and constant woman? Never!
Ugly old crones, possibly – now they might be faithful. But
you're as likely to run into a cat with horns, or a white
blackbird, as a faithful woman!

POPOVA. So tell me, sir – in your opinion, just who is faithful and constant in love? Men, you say?

SMIRNOV. Yes, men, of course!

POPOVA. Men! (*With a bitter laugh.*) Faithful and constant in love! Well, that's a new one. (*Heatedly.*) What gives you the right to say that? Men, faithful and constant? As far as that goes, I'll say this much – the best man I've ever known was my late husband. And I loved him passionately, with all my being, as only an intelligent young woman can love. I gave him my youth, my happiness, my life, my fortune – I lived and breathed for him alone, worshipped him like an idol... And... and... well? What then? This best of men, in the most shameless manner, betrayed me every step of the way! After his death I found a box full of love letters in his desk, and while he was still alive – oh, what terrible memories! – he would abandon me for weeks at a time, carry on with other women right in front of my eyes. He was unfaithful to me, squandered my money, made a joke of my feelings for him... Yet despite all that, I still loved him and was faithful to him. What's more, even though he's dead now, I've remained faithful and constant to him. I've buried myself within these four walls, and I shall wear these widow's weeds until the day I die.

SMIRNOV (*with a contemptuous laugh*). Widow's weeds? What do you take me for? D'you think I don't know why you're in that black get-up, why you've buried yourself away like this? Oh, come on now! It's so mysterious, so romantic, isn't it just. Some army cadet or would-be poet'll pass under your window and think: 'Here lives Tamara, the woman of mystery, buried alive for love of her husband.' It's a well-worn trick.

POPOVA (*exploding*). What! How dare you speak like that to me!

SMIRNOV. You've buried yourself alive, but you haven't forgotten to powder your nose.

POPOVA. How dare you address me in that manner!

SMIRNOV. And you needn't bother shouting at me, madam, I'm not one of your lackeys. I'm just calling a spade a spade. I'm not a woman, so I say what I mean, straight out. There's no need to shout.

POPOVA. It's you doing all the shouting, not me. Why don't you just leave me in peace?

SMIRNOV. Give me my money, then, and I'll go.

POPOVA. I'm not giving you any money!

SMIRNOV. Oh yes, you are!

POPOVA. Just for spite, you're not getting a single kopeck! So now you can leave me in peace.

SMIRNOV. Madam, I'm not your husband or your fiancé, I don't have that pleasure, so I'll thank you not to make a scene. (*Sits down.*) I don't like it.

POPOVA (*gasps, enraged*). You're sitting down?

SMIRNOV. I am.

POPOVA. Look, will you please leave!

SMIRNOV. Hand over my money! (*Aside.*) I'm absolutely raging! Spitting mad!

POPOVA. I've no wish to converse with such an impudent wretch. Now, if you don't mind, get out of my house! (*After a pause.*) You're not moving?

SMIRNOV. No.

POPOVA. No?

SMIRNOV. No.

POPOVA. Right, then. (*Rings.*)

LUKA *enters*.

Luka, show this gentleman out.

LUKA (*goes up to* SMIRNOV). Now then, sir, if you don't mind, you'd better go – when you're told…

SMIRNOV (*leaping to his feet*). Shut up, you! Who d'you think you're talking to? I'll make mincemeat of you!

LUKA (*clutching at his heart*). Oh, saints preserve us! (*Slumps into an armchair.*) Oh, I'm not well, this is terrible – I can't breathe!

POPOVA. Where's Dasha? Dasha! (*Shouts.*) Dasha! Pelageya! Dasha! (*Rings.*)

LUKA. Oh! They're all gone, ma'am – berry-picking. There's nobody in the house. Oh, I feel terrible! Water, please!

POPOVA. Look, just clear off, will you!

SMIRNOV. It wouldn't kill you to be a bit more polite.

POPOVA (*clenching her fists and stamping her feet*). Peasant! Ill-mannered oaf! You… you… bear! Monster!

SMIRNOV. What? What did you call me?

POPOVA. You're a bear, sir! A monster!

SMIRNOV (*advancing towards her*). And what gives you the right to insult me?

POPOVA. Yes, I'm insulting you, so what? D'you think I'm afraid of you?

SMIRNOV. And you think, just because you're one of these romantic creatures, you can get away with insulting me? Right, then – it's pistols!

LUKA. Saints above! Water!

SMIRNOV. A duel to the death!

POPOVA. You think because you've got big fists and can roar like a bull, I'm afraid of you? You great lout!

SMIRNOV. That's it, then – a duel! I don't let anybody insult me, weaker sex or no weaker sex!

POPOVA (*trying to shout him down*). Bear! Bear! Bear!

SMIRNOV. Yes, it's high time we set aside the prejudice that only men are obliged to give satisfaction for insults. You want equality, madam? Damn it, you'll get equality! Pistols at twenty paces!

POPOVA. A shooting match? Fine!

SMIRNOV. Right here and now!

POPOVA. Perfect! My husband left a brace of pistols, I'll fetch them this instant. (*Makes to hurry out, turns back.*) I'm going to enjoy putting a bullet into that thick skull of yours, damn you! (*Goes out.*)

SMIRNOV. I'll bring her down like a sitting duck! I'm no silly little boy, no moonstruck puppy dog – as far as I'm concerned, there's no such thing as the weaker sex!

LUKA. Oh, sir, kind sir! (*Falls to his knees.*) Have mercy on us, sir! Have pity on this old man, sir, and go away, please! First you scare us half to death, and now you're getting ready to shoot us!

SMIRNOV (*ignoring him*). A shooting match, now there's your equal rights, your emancipation! Equality of the sexes, right there – I'll shoot her as a matter of principle! But what a woman! (*Mimics her.*) 'I'll put a bullet into that thick skull of yours, damn you!' What a woman! Fired up, eyes blazing – and she accepts my challenge! Honest to God, she's like nothing I've ever seen.

LUKA. Oh, please, sir, go away, and I'll pray for you all my days!

SMIRNOV. What a woman! Now this I understand – a real woman, the genuine article, not some milk-and-water, simpering ninny, but a regular firebrand, a skyrocket! It'll be a shame to kill her.

LUKA (*weeping*). Oh, sir, kind sir – please go away!

SMIRNOV. I've taken a positive liking to her. Positively! Dimples notwithstanding. I'm even ready to let her off the money she owes me. And I'm not angry any more. An amazing woman!

POPOVA (*enters with the pistols*). Now, here are the pistols. Before we start, I'd be obliged if you'd show me how to fire them. I've never held a pistol before.

LUKA. Oh, Lord, have mercy on us! I'll go and find the gardener and the coachman. What's brought this disaster down on us, I don't know… (*Goes out.*)

SMIRNOV (*examines the pistols*). Actually, there are several types of pistol. For example, there's the Mortimer Special duelling pistol, with percussion caps. What you've got here are triple-action Smith & Wesson revolvers, with shell extraction and central firing… Top-notch weapons! A pair like these'll set you back ninety roubles, minimum. Anyway, you hold the pistol like this… (*Aside.*) Those eyes! Those eyes! Incendiary, what a woman!

POPOVA. Like this?

SMIRNOV. Yes, like that. Then you cock the hammer, and aim, like so. Keep your head back! And stretch your arm out – hold it straight out, that's it. Then with your finger, just squeeze this little thing here, simple as that. Important rule – don't get flustered, and don't be in a hurry. Watch your hand doesn't shake.

POPOVA. Fine. It's not convenient, shooting indoors – we'd better go out into the garden.

SMIRNOV. Right. But I ought to tell you now, I'll be firing into the air.

POPOVA. Oh, that's all I need! Why?

SMIRNOV. Because… Because… Look, that's my business.

POPOVA. Lost your nerve, have you? Eh? Oh no, sir, you're not worming your way out of this. Now if you don't mind, just follow me. I'll get no rest till I put a bullet into your brain – into that thick skull of yours which I detest! Got cold feet, have you?

SMIRNOV. Yes, I have.

POPOVA. Liar! Why don't you want to fight?

SMIRNOV. Because… Because I… Because I like you…

POPOVA (*laughs derisively*). He likes me! He has the gall to say he likes me! (*Points to the door.*) Just go, while you can.

SMIRNOV *silently lays down the revolver, picks up his cap and moves off. At the door he stops, and the two stand looking at each other without speaking, for half a minute or so. Eventually he speaks, and tentatively approaches* POPOVA.

SMIRNOV. Listen… Are you still angry? I mean, I'm furious too, damn it, but you need to understand… How can I put it? You see, the fact of the matter is, in this sort of business… When you get right down to it… (*Shouts.*) Oh, what the hell, it's not my fault if I like you! (*Grabs hold of the back of a chair, which cracks and breaks.*) Damn it, this furniture of yours is falling apart! Anyway, I like you! Do you understand? I think… I think I'm in love.

POPOVA. Get away from me! I hate you!

SMIRNOV. Oh, God, what a woman! I've never seen anything like it! I'm lost! Done for! Like a mouse caught in a trap!

POPOVA. Get back, or I'll shoot!

SMIRNOV. Go ahead and shoot! You can't imagine how happy I'd be to die, with those wonderful eyes gazing down at me, to be shot by a revolver gripped in that soft little velvety hand… I'm going mad! Just think – make up your mind now, because if I leave here, we'll never see each other again! Make up your mind. I'm a nobleman, thoroughly respectable, worth ten thousand a year. Toss a coin in the air, I can put a bullet right through it. I have a first-class stable. How would you fancy being my wife?

POPOVA (*indignant, brandishes her revolver*). Pistols! At twenty paces!

SMIRNOV. I'm losing my mind! This makes no sense whatsoever… (*Shouts.*) Hey, you, fellow! Some water!

POPOVA (*shouts*). Outside! Twenty paces!

SMIRNOV. I've gone mad, fallen for her like some half-witted schoolboy!

*Seizes her hand, she cries out in pain.*

I love you! (*Falls to his knees.*) I love you, as I've never loved anybody before. I've dumped twelve women, nine have dumped me, but not one of them have I loved the way I love you. I've turned to jelly, gone all sickly-sweet and soppy. I'm down on my knees like an idiot, offering you my hand. Shameful! Disgraceful! I haven't been in love for five years, I made a vow to myself I wouldn't, and suddenly I'm head over heels, back in harness again! Here, I'm giving you my hand – yes or no? Do you want it or don't you? Right... (*Gets up and walks quickly over to the door.*)

POPOVA. Wait!

SMIRNOV (*stops*). Well?

POPOVA. Nothing. Just go. No, wait... Oh, go away, go on... I hate you! Or no, don't go... Oh, if you knew how angry I am, I'm raging! (*Flings her revolver onto the table.*) My fingers are all swollen from this damned thing! (*Rips up a handkerchief in her rage.*) Well, what are you standing there for? Clear off!

SMIRNOV. Goodbye.

POPOVA. Yes, yes – go! (*Shouts.*) Where are you going? Wait... Oh, all right, just go. Oh, I'm so angry! Don't come near me! Don't even...

SMIRNOV (*goes up to her*). And I'm so angry at myself. Falling in love, like a silly schoolboy! Down on my knees! I'm breaking out in a cold sweat! (*Coarsely.*) In love with you? That's all I need! I've got the interest to pay tomorrow, the haymaking's just started, and here you are...(*Seizes her around the waist.*) I'll never forgive myself...

POPOVA. Get away from me! Take your hands off me! I... I... hate you! Twenty... paces... (*A prolonged kiss.*)

LUKA *enters carrying an axe, accompanied by the* GARDENER *holding a rake, and the* COOK *with a pitchfork, and several* WORKMEN *armed with staves, etc.*

LUKA (*seeing the couple kissing*). Saints preserve us!

*A pause.*

POPOVA (*modestly lowering her eyes*). Oh, Luka... Tell them in the stables... no oats for Toby today.

*Curtain.*

# THE PROPOSAL

*A farce in one act*

**Characters**

STEPAN STEPANOVICH CHUBUKOV, *a landowner*

NATALYA STEPANOVNA, *his daughter, aged twenty-five*

IVAN VASILIEVICH LOMOV, *a neighbouring landowner, in robust good health, but a chronic hypochondriac*

*The action takes place in the drawing room of* CHUBUKOV's *country house.*

LOMOV *enters, wearing a frock coat and white gloves.* CHUBUKOV *goes over to greet him warmly.*

CHUBUKOV. Goodness me, if it isn't my dearest friend! Ivan Vasilievich, I'm absolutely delighted! (*Shakes his hand.*) Heavens, what a surprise! How are you keeping?

LOMOV. Fine, thank you. And yourself, how are you?

CHUBUKOV. Oh, getting along, my angel, thanks to your prayers and all that. Sit down, have a seat, please do. It's not a good thing, dear heart, to forget one's neighbours, eh? But what's all this? Frock coat, white gloves – why so formal? I mean, you're surely not going somewhere else, my precious?

LOMOV. No, just to see you, dear sir.

CHUBUKOV. Yes, but the frock coat, man, all the trimmings – anyone would think it was Christmas!

LOMOV. Well, you see, the thing is... (*Takes him by the arm.*) My dear Stepan Stepanovich, I've come to trouble you for a favour. This isn't the first time I've been privileged to approach you for assistance, and in the past you've always... well, you know... I'm sorry, this isn't easy... If I could have a drink of water, dear sir... (*Takes a drink.*)

CHUBUKOV (*aside*). He's after money. Well, he's had it! (*Aloud.*) Tell me, my lovely – what is it?

LOMOV. The thing is... what I mean... Stepan Stepanovich... Good sir... My dear... Oh, Lord, I'm getting all worked up... You see what a state I'm in... The thing is... I mean, you're the only one who can help me, though God knows I don't deserve it, and I've absolutely no right to count on your assistance either...

CHUBUKOV. Stop beating about the bush, dear fellow! Spit it out! Well?

LOMOV. Yes, of course... in a minute... The fact is... Well, actually, I've come to ask for the hand of your daughter, Natalya Stepanovna, in marriage...

CHUBUKOV (*ecstatic*). Gracious me! Ivan Vasilievich! Say that again, I'm not sure I heard right!

LOMOV. Sir, I have the honour to ask for...

CHUBUKIN (*interrupting him*). My dearest friend! I'm so pleased – absolutely thrilled, delighted, and all that! (*Warmly embraces him.*) I've been wanting this for ages. It's been my greatest wish, always... (*Sheds a tear.*) I've always loved you, dear heart, like my very own son. God bless you both with good counsel and love and all that – oh, yes, it's what I've always wanted! But what am I standing here for, like an idiot? I'm overcome with joy, absolutely overcome. From the bottom of my heart, I... I'll go and call Natasha, and all that...

LOMOV (*deeply moved*). Dear Stepan Stepanovich, tell me – do you think I can count on her acceptance?

CHUBUKOV. What, a handsome fellow like you, and she'd turn you down? She's probably in love with you already, head over heels and all that... I'll be back in a minute... (*Goes out.*)

LOMOV (*alone*). It's so cold. I'm shaking like a leaf, as if I was sitting an exam or something. Make your mind up, that's the main thing. I mean, if you keep putting it off, dithering, mulling it over, waiting for the ideal match, true love or whatever, you'll never get married at all. Brrr – it's so cold! Natalya Stepanovna is an excellent housekeeper, not bad looking, well educated – what more do I need? But with all this excitement, I'm starting to get a buzzing in my ears. (*Takes a drink of water.*) I really should get married. In the first place, I'm already thirty-five – at a critical stage, as they say. In the second place, I need a bit of order and regularity in my life. I've got a heart condition, constant palpitations, I'm easily irritated, and I worry terribly all the time... I mean, this very minute my lips are trembling, and I've got a nervous tic in my right eye. Worst of all is sleep. No sooner

do I lie down in bed and start nodding off, than I get some
sort of stabbing pain in my left side that shoots straight up to
my shoulder and into my head. I spring out of bed like a
madman, pace the floor for a bit, then lie back down. And the
instant I start to drop off – bang! There goes my side again!
And it's like that twenty times a night…

NATALYA STEPANOVNA *enters*.

NATALYA. Goodness me, it's you! Papa said it was some
merchant or other, to pick up some goods. Well, how are
you, Ivan Vasilievich?

LOMOV. Very well, thank you, dear Natalya Stepanovna.

NATALYA. You'll have to excuse me, in this apron and
housecoat – we've been shelling peas for drying. It's ages
since we've seen you – why's that? Sit down, do, please…

*They sit down.*

Will you have some lunch?

LOMOV. No, thank you – I've already eaten.

NATALYA. Or if you want to smoke… here's some matches.
Isn't the weather lovely? We'd so much rain yesterday the
workers couldn't do a thing the whole day. Have you
managed to cut much hay? Believe it or not, I was so keen to
get started I cut the whole meadow, and now I'm worried in
case it all rots. I'd have been better waiting. Anyway, what's
all this? A frock coat? That's new – are you going to a ball or
something? It suits you very well, by the way, but what's the
fancy dress for?

LOMOV (*agitated*). Well, you see, dear Natalya Stepanovna…
The thing is, I've made up my mind to ask you… to… to hear
me out… I mean, you'll no doubt be surprised, and possibly
even angry, but I… (*Aside.*) It's terribly cold in here!

NATALYA. What is it? Well?

LOMOV. I'll try and keep it short. Dear Natalya Stepanovna,
as you are aware, I've had the great privilege of knowing

your family a very long time, since I was a boy, in fact. My late aunt and her husband, from whom, as you know, I inherited my land, always had the most profound respect for your father, and dear departed mother. The Lomovs and the Chubukovs have always been on the friendliest of terms – virtually family, one might say. Moreover, as you well know, my property very closely adjoins yours. And if I might remind you, my Ox Meadow actually borders your birch grove.

NATALYA. Excuse me, but I really must stop you there. You say *your* Ox Meadow. Is it actually yours?

LOMOV. It is, dear lady.

NATALYA. Well, that's rich! Ox Meadow is ours, not yours.

LOMOV. No no, dear Natalya Stepanovna – it's mine.

NATALYA. That's a new one on me. Since when has it been yours?

LOMOV. Since when? I'm talking about Ox Meadow, which forms a wedge between your birch trees and Burnt Marsh.

NATALYA. Yes, yes, that's right. And it's ours.

LOMOV. No, you're mistaken, dear Natalya Stepanovna. It's mine.

NATALYA. Think again, Ivan Vasilievich! When did it become yours?

LOMOV. When? It's always been ours, as far back as I remember.

NATALYA. Oh, this is ridiculous!

LOMOV. It's all down on paper, dear Natalya Stepanovna. There was some dispute about Ox Meadow at one time, that's true, but everybody knows it's mine now. There's no argument. If you'll let me explain, my aunt's grandmother handed over that meadow, rent-free and without limit of time, for your father's grandfather's peasants to use, because they made bricks for her. Your father's grandfather's peasants had the use of it free of charge for about forty years, and came to regard it as their own. And then, after the Emancipation...

NATALYA. That's not how it was at all! My grandfather, and great-grandfather took it for granted that their land ran right up to the edge of Burnt Marsh, which means that Ox Meadow is ours, end of story. I don't understand you at all and this is really annoying.

LOMOV. I can show you the papers, Natalya Stepanovna.

NATALYA. No, you're joking, surely, or trying to make a fool of me. Some surprise this is! We've owned this land for near enough three hundred years, and now he tells us it's not ours? Well, I'm sorry, Ivan Vasilievich, but I can't believe what I'm hearing. I'm not that bothered about the meadow, it's ten acres or so, worth about maybe three hundred roubles, but what really upsets me is the injustice of it all. You can say what you like, but I can't abide unfairness!

LOMOV. No, hear me out, please! Your father's grandfather's peasants, if I may respectfully remind you, used to make bricks for my aunt's grandmother. And my aunt's grandmother wanted to do them a good turn...

NATALYA. Grandfather, grandmother, aunt – I don't get any of this. The meadow's ours, and that's that!

LOMOV. It's mine!

NATALYA. It's ours! You can argue till you're blue in the face, dress up in as many frock coats as you can lay claim to, it's still ours, ours, ours! I don't want anything of yours, but I'm not letting go of what's ours, so there!

LOMOV. Natalya Stepanovna, I don't even need Ox Meadow, but it's the principle of the thing. I mean, I'll quite happily make you a present of it, if you want.

NATALYA. And I can make you a present of it, because it's mine! This is absurd, Ivan Vasilievich, to say the very least. Up until now we've always regarded you as a good neighbour, and friend. Why, last year we kept letting you use our threshing machine, which meant we couldn't get our own harvest threshed until November! And now you're treating us like gypsies! Making me a present of my own land, indeed! Well, excuse me, but that isn't very neighbourly. Damned cheek, I'd call it!

LOMOV. So you see me as some sort of land-grabber? Well, my dear lady, I'll have you know I've never grabbed anybody's land – that's something I can't be accused of, and I won't stand for it... (*Goes quickly over to the carafe and takes a drink of water.*) Ox Meadow is mine!

NATALYA. That's a lie, it's ours!

LOMOV. Mine!

NATALYA. That's a lie, and I'll prove it! I'm sending my men over to cut it this very day!

LOMOV. You what?

NATALYA. My men'll be in that meadow today!

LOMOV. Then I'll just have to kick them out, won't I!

NATALYA. You wouldn't dare!

LOMOV (*clutching at his heart*). Ox Meadow's mine, do you hear? Mine!

NATALYA. Stop shouting, please! You can rant and rave all you like in your own house, but in this house kindly exercise a bit of decorum.

LOMOV. If it wasn't for the fact, dear lady, that I'm having the most excruciating palpitations, and if the veins weren't throbbing in my temples, believe me, I'd be speaking to you quite differently! (*Shouts.*) Ox Meadow is mine!

NATALYA. Ours!

LOMOV. Mine!

NATALYA. Ours!

CHUBUKOV *enters.*

CHUBUKOV. What's all this? What's all the shouting about?

NATALYA. Papa, kindly inform this gentleman who owns Ox Meadow – him or us?

CHUBUKOV (*to* LOMOV) Why, we do, my angel, of course.

LOMOV. I beg your pardon, Stepan Stepanovich, but how exactly does it come to be yours? Let's at least be sensible about this. My aunt's grandmother gave it to your grandfather's peasants, rent-free, on a temporary basis. They had the use of that land for about forty years, and came to regard it as their own. So when the Emancipation happened...

CHUBUKOV. Now hold on, my precious. You're forgetting that in point of fact those peasants didn't pay anything to your grandmother and all that, because the meadow was already the subject of a dispute, et cetera, et cetera. And nowadays even the dogs know the land belongs to us. You've obviously never seen the map!

LOMOV. But I can prove it's mine!

CHUBUKOV. No, you can't, my sweeting.

LOMOV. Yes, I can!

CHUBUKOV. Goodness me, why do you need to shout? Shouting proves nothing. I don't want any of your property, and I don't intend to give up any of mine. Why should I? If push comes to shove, my darling, and you're spoiling for a fight over that meadow, et cetera, I'd rather give it to the peasants than you. So there!

LOMOV. I don't get this at all. What right have you to give away someone else's property?

CHUBUKOV. Kindly allow me to be the judge of what rights I have or don't have. And let me tell you, young man, I'm not in the habit of being spoken to in that fashion, et cetera. I'm twice your age, my young fellow, and I expect you to address me with a measure of respect, and so forth.

LOMOV. What sort of an idiot do you take me for? D'you think I'm a fool? You're telling me my land belongs to you, and I'm supposed to take all this calmly and make polite conversation about it? Decent neighbours don't do this sort of thing, Stepan Stepanovich! You're not a neighbour, you're a shameless land-grabber!

CHUBUKOV. What? What did you say?

NATALYA. Papa, send the men out to cut the meadow right this minute!

CHUBUKOV (*to* LOMOV). Excuse me, sir – what did you actually say?

NATALYA. Ox Meadow's ours, and I'm not giving in, I'm not, absolutely not!

LOMOV. Well, we'll just see about that. I'll have the law on you, I'll prove it's mine!

CHUBUKOV. The law? Go right ahead, take us to court, my dear sir, sue us, and all that! Just try! I know your sort, yes indeed, just waiting for the chance, just itching to go to court and suchlike! Suing people at the drop of a hat, that's your style. Litigation-happy, your whole family's the same, all of them!

LOMOV. I'll thank you not to insult my family, sir! The Lomovs have always been honest people – not one of them has ever been charged with embezzlement, unlike that precious uncle of yours!

CHUBUKOV. And you Lomovs are a bunch of lunatics, the whole lot of you!

NATALYA. All of them, yes, every last one!

CHUBUKOV. Your grandfather drank like a fish, and your aunt, the younger one, what's her name, Nastasya Mikhailovna, yes – she ran off with an architect, and all that…

LOMOV. And your mother was deformed… (*Clutches his heart.*) Oh, I've a stabbing pain in my side… and a splitting headache… Oh, God, water!

CHUBUKOV. And your father was a card sharp and a notorious glutton!

NATALYA. And that aunt of yours was an interfering old busybody!

LOMOV. Oh, my left leg's gone numb! And you're a conniving dog, sir. Oh, my heart! Everybody knows how just before the elections, you went round… Oh, now I've got flashing lights in front of my eyes! Where's my hat?

NATALYA. What damned cheek! This is shameful, absolutely disgusting!

CHUBUKOV. You're nothing but a snake-in-the-grass, sir, a vile, bare-faced hypocrite! Yes, indeed!

LOMOV. My hat, there it is… Oh, my heart… Let me out of here! Where's the door? Oh! I think I'm dying! (*Goes over to the door.*) I can scarcely lift my foot over the doorstep!

CHUBUKOV (*calling after him*). And you needn't bother darkening it ever again, with your foot or anything else!

NATALYA. Yes, go right ahead and sue us – we'll see what happens!

LOMOV *staggers out.*

CHUBUKOV. To hell with him! (*Pacing the floor, agitated.*)

NATALYA. Nasty creature! That's what we get for trusting our nice neighbours!

CHUBUKOV. Miserable wretch! Pea-brained scarecrow!

NATALYA. Monstrous! Steals somebody else's land, then has the cheek to start swearing at us!

CHUBUKOV. And this freak, this blundering ninny, has the effrontery to come round here with a proposal, no less! I mean, really – a proposal!

NATALYA. What proposal?

CHUBUKOV. Well, what d'you think? He rode over here to propose to you.

NATALYA. A proposal? To me? Why didn't you tell me this before?

CHUBUKOV. What d'you think he was all dressed up for? Damned stuffed shirt! Weed!

NATALYA. Me? Propose to me? Oh! (*Slumps into an armchair, groans.*) Get him back here! Get him back! Oh, God! Get him back!

CHUBUKOV. Get who back?

NATALYA. Hurry up, hurry! I'm going to be sick. Get him back! (*Almost hysterical.*)

CHUBUKOV. What is it? What's the matter with you? (*Clutches his head.*) This is a nightmare! I'm going to shoot myself – or hang myself! They've driven me to it!

NATALYA. I'm dying! Get him back, I tell you!

CHUBUKOV. Aargh! All right, I'm going, I'm going – just stop howling! (*Runs out.*)

NATALYA (*alone, groans*). Oh God, what have we done? Bring him back, please – bring him back!

CHUBUKOV (*running back in*). He's coming back right now, and so forth – damn the man! Aargh! But you'd better talk to him – I mean, really, I'd rather not.

NATALYA (*groans*). Get him back here!

CHUBUKOV (*shouts*). He's coming, I've told you! Dear God, what a responsibility – to be landed with an unmarried daughter! I'll cut my throat! I definitely will! We swear at the man, insult him, kick him out of the house, and it's all down to you, it's your fault!

NATALYA. It was not, it was yours!

CHUBUKOV. So it's my fault, is it now?

LOMOV *appears in the doorway.*

Right, on you go – he's all yours! (*Goes out.*)

LOMOV *enters, clearly exhausted.*

LOMOV. I've got the most frightful palpitations... I can't feel my leg... I have a stabbing pain in my side...

NATALYA. I'm sorry, Ivan Vasilievich, things got a little out of hand... Actually I remember now – Ox Meadow does belong to you...

LOMOV. My heart's pounding like mad... That meadow's mine... I've got a nervous tic in both eyes...

NATALYA. Anyway, the meadow's yours – definitely. Won't you have a seat?

*They sit down.*

We were in the wrong.

LOMOV. It's the principle of the thing. I'm not bothered about the land, but it's the principle.

NATALYA. The principle, yes, right. Let's change the subject.

LOMOV. All the more so because I have proof. My aunt's grandmother gave the land to your father's grandfather's peasants...

NATALYA. Yes, yes, that's enough of that. (*Aside.*) I don't know where to begin. (*Aloud.*) So, are you going out hunting soon?

LOMOV. Yes, once the harvest's in, dear Natalya Stepanovna. Grouse shooting, I think. Oh, you haven't heard? You wouldn't believe it, the rotten luck I have, honestly. You know my dog Nimrod? He's gone lame!

NATALYA. Oh, that's awful! What happened?

LOMOV. I don't know. He must've twisted something, or else the other dogs attacked him... (*Sighs.*) He's my best dog, too – not to mention the money. I mean, I paid Mironov a hundred and twenty-five roubles for that dog!

NATALYA. You were robbed, Ivan Vasilievich!

LOMOV. Not at all – I think he was a bargain. Nimrod is a superb dog.

NATALYA. Papa paid eighty-five roubles for our dog Roly, and he's a much better dog than your Nimrod.

LOMOV. Better than my Nimrod? You must be joking! (*Laughs*.) Roly better than my Nimrod!

NATALYA. Of course he's better! Roly's still not lost his puppy fat, but the way he stands and points, his movements – you won't find a better dog anywhere, not even in Volchanetsky's pack!

LOMOV. I beg your pardon, Natalya Stepanovna, but you seem to be forgetting – Roly has an overbite, and a dog with an overbite can't grip anything.

NATALYA. An overbite? Since when?

LOMOV. I assure you – his lower jaw is shorter than the upper.

NATALYA. What, have you measured it?

LOMOV. Yes, I have. He'll do all right in the chase, obviously, but when he tries to retrieve something, well…

NATALYA. In the first place, our Roly is a top-quality purebred animal, with a flawless pedigree, whereas God only knows what spawned that grubby-looking piebald freak of yours. Besides which, he's old and ugly, like a clapped-out old nag!

LOMOV. Old? I wouldn't take five of your Rolys for him! Am I hearing right? Nimrod is a proper dog – Roly's just a… oh, really, there's no point in arguing, this is ludicrous. Dogs like your Roly are a drug on the market – every kennel's swarming with them. Worth twenty-five roubles at the outside.

NATALYA. I don't know what's the matter with you today, Ivan Vasilievich, you're so downright contradictory. First you claim Ox Meadow's yours, next it's Nimrod's better than Roly. I can't abide people who won't say what they really believe. I mean, you know perfectly well that our Roly's a hundred times better than that stupid Nimrod of yours, so why say the opposite?

LOMOV. Well, obviously, Natalya Stepanovna, you think I'm either blind or a fool. Why can't you see it? Roly has an overbite!

NATALYA. No, he hasn't!

LOMOV. Yes, he has!

NATALYA (*shouts*). No, he hasn't!

LOMOV. Don't shout at me, my dear lady.

NATALYA. Then don't talk nonsense! I've never heard such utter tripe! Your Nimrod's on his last legs, it's time he was put down, and you're comparing him with Roly?

LOMOV. I'm sorry, I can't take any more of this – I'm having palpitations.

NATALYA. Yes, well, I've noticed that people who make most noise about hunting generally know very little about it.

LOMOV. Enough, dear lady, for pity's sake – my heart's about to burst... (*Shouts.*) Shut... up!

NATALYA. No, I'm not going to shut up until you admit that Roly's a hundred times better than your Nimrod!

LOMOV. He's a hundred times worse! I wish your Roly would drop dead! Oh, my head's throbbing... my eyes... my shoulder...

NATALYA. Actually that idiotic Nimrod of yours doesn't even need to be put down – he's more dead than alive already!

LOMOV (*in tears*). Shut up! I'm having a heart attack!

NATALYA. I won't shut up!

CHUBUKOV *enters*.

CHUBUKOV. What's going on?

NATALYA. Papa, tell the truth – hand on heart – which is the better dog, our Roly or his Nimrod?

LOMOV. Stepan Stepanovich, please – just one thing. Has Roly got an overbite or not? Yes or no?

CHUBUKOV. Well, what if he has? Who cares? There isn't a finer dog anywhere for miles around, and all that.

LOMOV. But surely my Nimrod's better? Tell the truth, now.

CHUBUKOV. Don't get upset, my precious. If you'll allow me... Your dog Nimrod has his points, I grant you. He's a pedigree animal, good strong legs, solid hindquarters, and suchlike. But if you really want to know, my lovely – that dog of yours suffers from two essential defects: he's too old, and he's got a short muzzle.

LOMOV. Excuse me, I'm having palpitations again... Now, let's look at the facts. If you remember, at the Maruskys' Green, my Nimrod went neck-and-neck with the Count's Swinger, while your Roly was a good half a mile behind.

CHUBUKOV. He was only behind because the Count's groom laid into him a whip!

LOMOV. And for good reason – the dogs were supposed to be chasing a fox, and your Roly was worrying a sheep!

CHUBUKOV. That's a lie, sir! I've got a very short fuse, my darling, so don't let's argue any more. He whipped him because basically nobody can stand the sight of another man's dog. So there! Positively detest them, in fact. And you're no exception, my dear sir! Indeed, no. I mean, the instant you spot that somebody's dog is better than your Nimrod, right away you wade in with this, that, and the other, et cetera... Oh yes, d'you think I don't remember?

LOMOV. And I remember too!

CHUBUKOV (*mimicking him*). And I remember too! Well, go on – what do you remember?

LOMOV. My heart... palpitations... My leg's gone numb... I can't...

NATALYA (*mocking*). Palpitations! What kind of a sportsman are you? You should be stretched out on the kitchen stove, squashing cockroaches, not chasing foxes. Palpitations, yet!

CHUBUKOV. Yes, some sportsman, right enough! You should be at home, nursing your palpitations, not tearing around on horseback! All well and good if you actually did hunt, but the only reason you get on a horse is to start arguments and annoy other people's dogs, and all that. Now, I've got a bad temper, so let's put a stop to this. You're no sportsman, and that's all there is to it!

LOMOV. Oh, and I suppose you are? You only hunt so you can suck up to the Count, and scheme behind people's backs... Oh, my heart! A schemer, that's what you are!

CHUBUKOV. What? You're calling me a schemer? (*Shouts.*) Shut up!

LOMOV. Schemer!

CHUBUKOV. Impertinent young pup!

LOMOV. And you're an old rat! A Jesuit!

CHUBUKOV. If you don't shut up this minute I'll fetch my rusty old shotgun and bring you down like a partridge! Windbag!

LOMOV. It's common knowledge that... Oh, my heart! Your dear departed wife used to beat you up... Oh, my leg! My head's throbbing... Lights flashing in my eyes... I feel faint, I'm falling!

CHUBUKOV. And your housekeeper walks all over you!

LOMOV. Oh! Oh! My heart's bursting! My shoulder feels as if it's been torn off! What's happened to my shoulder? I'm dying! (*Slumps into an armchair.*) Get me a doctor! (*Faints.*)

CHUBUKOV. Crybaby! Milksop! Faker! God, I feel awful! (*Drinks some water.*) Absolutely awful!

NATALYA. Call yourself a sportsman? You don't even know how to sit on a horse! (*To* CHUBUKOV.) Papa, what's the matter with him? Papa! Look at him, Papa! (*Shrieks*.) Ivan Vasilievich! He's dead!

CHUBUKOV. I feel dreadful! I can't breathe! I need air!

NATALYA. He's dead! (*Tugs at* LOMOV's *sleeve*.) Ivan Vasilievich! Ivan Vasilievich! What have we done to him? He's dead! (*Slumps into an armchair.*) Get a doctor! We need a doctor! (*Hysterical*.)

CHUBUKOV. Oh! What is it? What's the matter with you?

NATALYA (*groans*). He's dead!... Dead!

CHUBUKOV. Who's dead? (*Looks over at* LOMOV.) Oh, my God – he *is* dead! Get me some water! Fetch the doctor! (*Puts a glass of water to* LOMOV's *lips*.) Here, drink this! No, he's not drinking... That means he's dead, and so forth... Oh, dear God, I'm the unluckiest man alive! Why don't I just put a bullet in my brain? Why haven't I cut my throat long before this? What am I waiting for? Give me a knife! Where's my pistol!

LOMOV *stirs*.

I think he's coming to... Here, have a sip of water...

LOMOV. My eyes... flashing lights.... fog... Where am I?

CHUBUKOV. Hurry up and get married, and... oh, to hell with you – yes, she accepts! (*Joins* LOMOV*'s hand to* NATALYA*'s*.) She's agreeable, and all that! You have my blessing, et cetera! Just leave me in peace!

LOMOV. Eh? What? (*Sits up*.) Who?

CHUBUKOV. She says yes! What are you waiting for? Kiss her, for God's sake! What the hell's up with the pair of you?

NATALYA (*groans*). He's alive... yes, yes, I accept...

CHUBUKOV. Kiss her!

LOMOV. Eh? Who? (*Kisses* NATALYA.) Delighted, I'm sure... I beg your pardon, but what's this all about? Oh, yes, I see now... My heart... my eyes... flashes... I'm so happy,

Natalya Stepanovna... (*Kisses her hand*.) My leg's gone to sleep...

NATALYA. And I... I'm happy too.

CHUBUKOV. Well, that's a weight off my shoulders... phew!

NATALYA. But you will admit now, won't you... that your Nimrod isn't as good as our Roly?

LOMOV. Better!

NATALYA. Worse!

CHUBUKOV. That's married bliss off to a good start! Champagne!

LOMOV. Better!

NATALYA. Worse! Worse! Worse!

CHUBUKOV (*trying to drown them out*). Champagne! Champagne!

*Curtain.*

# A TRAGIC FIGURE
# (FROM COUNTRY LIFE)

*A farce in one act*

**Characters**

IVAN IVANOVICH TOLKACHOV, *a family man*

ALEXEI ALEXEYEVICH MURASHKIN, *his friend*

*The action takes place in St Petersburg, in* MURASHKIN*'s apartment.*

MURASHKIN's *study, comfortably furnished.* MURASHKIN *is sitting at his writing table.* TOLKACHOV *enters, carrying a glass lamp-globe, a child's bicycle, three hatboxes, a large bundle of clothes, some bottles of beer in a bag, and a number of other small packages. He looks round him in a daze, before slumping exhausted onto a sofa.*

MURASHKIN. Ivan Ivanych! How nice to see you! Where on earth have you been?

TOLKACHOV (*gasping for breath*). Dear friend... I need a favour... If you'd be so kind... Please... Lend me your revolver... Till tomorrow... Please, dear friend, I'm begging you...

MURASHKIN. Why do you want a revolver?

TOLCHAKOV. Because I need one. Oh, God! A drink of water, please! Quick! I really need that revolver – I've got to ride through a wood tonight, in the dark... I mean, you never know... Be a good friend and help me out, for pity's sake!

MURASHKIN. That's nonsense, Ivan Ivanych. What the devil are you talking about? Dark wood, indeed! You're up to something, more like. I can see it in your face, you're up to no good. What's the matter with you? Are you ill?

TOLCHAKOV. Give me a minute, till I catch my breath. Oh, God, I'm completely shattered, it's a dog's life. My whole body, my brain – it feels as if they've made mincemeat of me! I can't stand it any more. Just be a good friend, and don't ask, don't press me for details. Give me that revolver – please!

MURASHKIN. Stop, stop, that's enough! Ivan Ivanych, pull yourself together, don't be such a crybaby. Really! And you a family man, a state councillor – shame on you!

TOLCHAKOV. Family man, what d'you mean, family man? I'm a martyr! A beast of burden, a slave, a serf, a vile wretch, still clinging on, waiting for God knows what, afraid to end it all! A dishrag, that's what I am, a numskull, a mindless idiot! What am I living for? Why? (*Jumps up*.) Come on, tell me, what's the point of it? This unremitting onslaught of moral and physical torments, eh? I mean, I can understand sacrificing yourself for a cause, that's all well and good, but a martyr to women's petticoats and lampshades, for God's sake – no! No, thank you kindly, ma'am! No, no, no! I've had enough! Enough!

MURASHKIN. Stop shouting, the neighbours can hear.

TOLCHAKOV. Let them hear, I don't care! If you won't give me a revolver, somebody else will. I'm already a dead man, I've made up my mind.

MURASHKIN. Look, you've torn off one of my buttons. Calm down, for goodness' sake. I still don't understand – is your life really so bad?

TOLCHAKOV. What? You're asking me that? Just let me tell you, then. Let me get it off my chest, and maybe I'll feel the better for it. Let's sit down. Right, listen... Oh, dear God, I can't get a breath! Let's take today as an example. Yes, we'll take today. As you well know, from ten to four I'm chained to my desk at the office. It's damnably hot and stuffy, flies everywhere, absolute bedlam. The secretary's on leave, Khrapov's gone off to get married, the office pond life are obsessed with dachas, love affairs, amateur dramatics. Everybody's half-asleep, exhausted, completely washed out, you can't get any sense out of them. The character filling in for the secretary is deaf in one ear, and in love, for heaven's sake. The clients are punch-drunk, running from one desk to the next, spitting mad and threatening violence. The whole place is in uproar, it's enough to make you shout for help. Sheer mayhem and confusion, it's like hell on earth. And the work itself is mind-numbing, same thing day after day: enquiry, referral, enquiry, referral – huge tidal waves of monotony. You feel as if your eyes were slowly crawling out of your head, do you know what I mean? Some water, please... You leave work exhausted, absolutely shattered, just looking forward to dinner at home and collapsing into bed. Hah, fat chance! You remember that you're the proud possessor of a dacha, a summer cottage, i.e., you're a slave, a dishrag, a snivelling nonentity, and an errand boy, by your leave, expected to rush around like a headless chicken, doing the family shop! Oh yes, there's a charming little routine in our dachas: if the husband has to go into town each day, then not only his wife, but every sun-loving parasite and his dog has the right to burden him with a mountain of errands. My wife demands I go to her dressmaker and give her a good ticking off because the bodice has turned out too full, and the shoulders are too narrow. Sonya needs a pair of shoes exchanged; my sister-in-law wants twenty kopecks' worth of crimson silk to match a pattern, and two-and-a-half metres of braid. Yes, just hold on and I'll read this out to you... (*Takes a note out of his pocket and reads*.) 'A lamp-globe; a pound of ham sausage; five kopecks' worth of cloves and cinnamon; castor oil for Misha; ten pounds of granulated sugar, and fetch the copper basin and the mortar for the sugar from home; carbolic acid; insect powder; ten kopecks' worth of face powder; twenty bottles of beer; vinegar essence and a size eighty-two corset for Mademoiselle Chanceau – ugh! And bring Misha's overcoat and galoshes from home.' That's the shopping list for my wife and family. Now the list for our dear friends and neighbours, to hell with the lot of them! It's Volodya Vlasin's name-day tomorrow, I have to buy a bicycle for him. Colonel Vikhrin's wife is in an interesting condition, so to speak, which means I'm obliged to make daily calls on the midwife, and invite her to pay a visit. And on and on and on it goes. I have five lists in my pocket, and a handkerchief full of knots. So, my dear friend, in the interval between leaving the office and catching the train, you have to run around town like a dog, your tongue hanging out – run non-stop, cursing your wretched life. From the shop to the chemist's, from the chemist's to the dressmaker, from the dressmaker to the delicatessen, then back to the chemist's. In one place you fall over; in another you lose your money; in a third, you forget to pay, so they chase after you and kick up hell; in a fourth, you accidentally step on some woman's skirt... phew! All this frantic haring around drives you crazy, you're coming apart at the seams, at night all your bones creak and you dream about crocodiles. And now, sir, the errands are done, everything's bought and paid for – tell me, how the devil am I supposed to parcel up all this stuff? I mean, for example, do I pack the heavy copper mortar along with the lamp-globe, or mix the carbolic with the tea? And how am I going to make one parcel out of all these beer bottles and that bicycle? It's the riddle of the Sphinx, mind-numbing, it makes no sense whatever! You can rack your brains till the cows come home, apply all your ingenuity, but in the long run you're bound to smash or spill something, and at the station, and in the carriage, you'll end up standing with your arms outstretched and your legs spread, trying to hang on to some parcel with your chin, covered in bags and boxes and all manner of rubbish. And the minute the train moves off, people'll start tossing your stuff all over the place, because you've put it down on their seats. They'll shout at you, calling for the conductor, threatening to have you thrown off, and what do you do then? You stand open-mouthed, like a whipped cur. And there's more to come. I'll finally arrive at the dacha, and what would be really welcome would be some reward for my labours, a decent drink and a bite to eat, topped off with a snooze – you'd think so, wouldn't you? Not a hope. My beloved spouse has been watching out for me for hours. You barely manage a mouthful of soup but she's going hell-for-leather at your humble servant, 'You're sure you don't fancy taking in that amateur theatre show, or the dance circle?' And you can't possibly refuse. You're a 'husband', and in dacha parlance, that word translates as 'dumb animal', a creature you can ride on or load up with baggage to your heart's content, without fear of intervention by the cruelty inspectors. So off you go to stare goggle-eyed at *Scandal in a Respectable Family*, or some other tenth-rate play, applauding when your wife tells you to, feeling your lifeblood draining away, expecting to have a seizure any second. And at the dance club you watch the dances, scanning the room to find likely partners for your wife, and if there aren't enough, you wind up doing the damn quadrille yourself. You take the floor with one Krivulya Ivanovna, no less, with a silly smile on your face, all the while thinking, 'How long, oh Lord, how long?' And after midnight, when you get home from the theatre or the dance, you're no longer a human being, you're more dead than alive, fit for nothing. But you've finally achieved your goal – you undress and get into bed. Wonderful, just close your eyes and go to sleep... so warm and cosy, sheer bliss, you know what I mean? The children in the next room have stopped whining, the wife's not there, your conscience is clear – it couldn't be better. You're just dozing off, and suddenly... and suddenly you hear... bzzz! Mosquitoes! (*Springs to his feet*.) Mosquitoes, God damn it! Damn and blast the little swines! (*Shakes his fist*.) Mosquitoes! Like the plague of Egypt, or the Spanish Inquisition! Bzzzz! This damn buzzing's so pathetic, so mournful, you'd think it was begging for forgiveness, till the vicious little devil bites you and you spend the next hour scratching. You smoke, you take a swipe at it, you cover your head – it's no use, there's no salvation. Finally you give up – to hell with it – let them tear you to bits. Go on, fill your boots, you greedy little buggers! And just when you've got used to the mosquitoes, along comes a new Egyptian plague. Your wife starts singing, yes, rehearsing ballads in the drawing room, accompanied by her gentleman friends. Tenors, for God's sake! They sleep all day and spend their nights tuning up for amateur concerts. God Almighty – tenors! That's a worse form of torture than mosquitoes, even! (*Sings*.) 'Oh, never say that thy young life is ended...' 'I stand before thee, yet again enchanted...' Dis-GUS-ting! They've drained the very soul out of me. To deaden the noise a bit, I try this little trick – tapping my finger on my head beside my ear. I carry on tapping like that till four in the morning, when the singers eventually disperse. Oh, some more water, friend, please! I can't go on... Well, anyway, sleep's out of the question – you get up at six, make a beeline for the station to catch the train. You run, afraid in case you miss it, through the mud, and fog, and freezing cold – brrr! And when you get to town, the whole rigmarole starts over again. I'm telling you, friend, that's the story of my miserable life – I wouldn't wish it on my worst enemy. It's made me ill, it really has. I can't breathe, I suffer from heartburn, I'm constantly jumpy, my digestion's shot to hell, I've got double vision... I've become totally neurotic, yes, I have... (*Looks round.*) Just between the two of us, I could do with seeing a psychiatrist. It's as if a bloody great black cloud has descended on me. You know, at times when I get annoyed or depressed, when the damn mosquitoes are biting or the tenors wailing, a red mist suddenly comes over me, I jump up and run round the house like a crazy person, shouting, 'I will have blood! Blood!' And you actually do feel like sticking a knife into somebody, or smashing a chair over their head. That's what this country life does to you. And you get no sympathy, nobody gives a damn, as if that's how it's meant to be. They think it's funny, but I mean, I'm alive, I've got a life, and I want to live too! This isn't some sort of farce, it's a tragedy! Look, if you're not going to give me that revolver, you might at least show a bit of sympathy!

MURASHKIN. I do – I do sympathise.

TOLKACHOV. Yes, I can see that... Anyway, goodbye. I have to get some sprats, and some sausage... after that, tooth powder, and then to the station.

MURASHKIN. So where exactly is the dacha you're staying in?

TOLKACHOV. Dead Man's Creek.

MURASHKIN (*delightedly*). Really? Listen, you don't happen to know somebody down there called Olga Finberg?

TOLKACHOV. Yes, I do. Quite well, in fact.

MURASHKIN. Honestly? Well, there's a coincidence. What a stroke of luck! And that's really kind of you...

TOLKACHOV. What are you talking about?

MURASHKIN. I have a tiny little favour to ask of you, my dear, good friend, if you wouldn't mind. Now, promise me you'll do it.

TOLKACHOV. Do what?

MURASHKIN. It's nothing, really, just for friendship's sake. Please, be a dear good fellow. First, give my regards to Olga Pavlovna, tell her I'm fit and well, and send her my love. Secondly, there's a little thing I'd like you to take her. She asked me to buy her a portable sewing machine, and I haven't got anybody to deliver it. If you'd take it down to her, that'd be a real kindness. Oh, and there's also this cage, with the canary... Just be careful with it, and don't break the little door... Why are you looking at me like that?

TOLKACHOV. A sewing machine... a canary in a cage... goldfinches, next, bloody chaffinches...

MURASHKIN. Ivan Ivanych, what's the matter? You've gone bright red, what is it?

TOLKACHOV (*stamping his feet*). Right, give me the sewing machine! Where's the damn birdcage? Climb on my back yourself, why don't you! Eat a man alive! Tear him apart! Beat him to a pulp! I will have blood! Blood! Blood!

MURASHKIN. Have you gone mad?

TOLKACHOV (*advancing towards him*). I will have blood! Blood!

MURASHKIN (*terrified*). He's gone mad! Petrushka! Marya! Where are you! Help! Save me!

TOLKACHOV (*chasing him round the room*). I'll have blood! Blood!

*Curtain.*

# THE WEDDING

*A play in one act*

## Characters

YEVDOKIM ZAKHAROVICH ZHIGALOV, *a retired civil servant*

NASTASYA TIMOFEYEVNA, *his wife*

DASHENKA, *their daughter*

EPAMINOND MAXIMOVICH APLOMBOV, *her fiancé*

FYODOR YAKOVLEVICH REVUNOV-KARAULOV, *a retired Navy Captain*

ANDREI ANDREYEVICH NYUNIN, *an insurance agent*

ANNA MARTYNOVNA ZMEYUKINA, *a midwife aged thirty, in a bright crimson dress*

IVAN MIKHAILOVICH YAT, *a telegraph clerk*

KHARLAMPY SPIRIDONOVICH DYMBA, *a Greek pastry cook*

DMITRY STEPANOVICH MOZGOVOY, *a sailor in the Volunteer Fleet*

ALEXEI ALEXEYEVICH MURASHKIN, *his friend*

BEST MAN

*Plus other young men, and servants.*

*The action takes place in a function room at a large restaurant.*

*A large, brightly lit room; a long table, laid for supper,*
WAITERS *in tailcoats bustling about. Offstage, an orchestra is playing the last part of a quadrille.* ZMEYUKINA *crosses the stage, followed by* YAT *and the* BEST MAN.

ZMEYUKINA. No, no, no!

YAT. Oh, come on, please – for pity's sake!

ZMEYUKINA. No, no, no!

BEST MAN (*hurrying after them*). Oh, this is impossible! Where are you going? You can't leave the floor, it's the *grand-ronde*! *S'il vous plaît* – please!

*They go out. Enter* NASTASYA *and* APLOMBOV.

NASTASYA. Oh, talk, talk, talk – go away and don't bother me. Get back in there and dance.

APLOMBOV. I'm not Spinoza, you know, and my head's spinning already, it's like trying to make pretzels with my feet! I'm a solid, respectable citizen, and I just don't enjoy these empty pleasures. Anyway, I'm not talking about the dancing. I'm sorry, *chère maman*, but I find some of your actions frankly incomprehensible. For instance, along with certain essential household items, you also promised that your daughter's dowry would include two lottery tickets. So where are they?

NASTASYA. I think I'm getting a headache. It must be the weather – surely a thaw coming on.

APLOMBOV. Don't try and talk your way out of it. I've just found out those tickets have been pawned. If you don't mind my saying, *maman*, that takes a bit of cheek. It's not out of selfishness – I don't need your tickets. But it's a matter of principle, and I won't let anybody make a fool of me. I've made your daughter a happy woman, but if you don't hand

over those tickets today, I'll have her for breakfast – I'm a
man of my word!

NASTASYA (*looking round the table and counting the places*).
One, two, three, four, five...

WAITER. Cook wants to know how you'd like the ice cream
served – with rum, madeira, or just on its own?

APLOMBOV. With rum. And tell your boss there's not enough
wine. Tell him to put out some *Haut Sauterne*. (*To
NASTASYA*.) You also promised there'd be a General
invited to the dinner. That was agreed, so where is he, then?

NASTASYA. I'm not to blame for that, my dear.

APLOMBOV. Well, who is?

NASTASYA. Andrei Andreyich – it's his fault. He was here
yesterday, and said he'd bring a General along with him – a
real one. (*Sighs*.) I don't suppose he could find one, or else
he'd have come. It's not meanness on our part, I assure you.
Nothing's too good for our darling daughter. You wanted a
General, that's fine by us.

APLOMBOV. And another thing... Everybody, including
yourself, knows that before I proposed to your darling
daughter, she was being courted by that telegraph clerk –
Yat, is it? So why has he been invited? Didn't it cross your
mind I might be annoyed?

NASTASYA. Oh... what's your name again? Epaminond
Maximych, yes – you've scarcely been married a day, and
you're already nagging Dashenka and me half to death. Dear
God, what'll it be like after a year? You go on and on, you
really do!

APLOMBOV. You don't like to hear the truth – that's it, isn't it?
Yes. Well, just treat people decently, that's all I want, some
decent treatment.

*At the back of the room, entering through one door and
exiting by another, couples dance the* grand-ronde, *led by the*
BEST MAN *and* DASHENKA. YAT *and* ZMEYUKINA,

*bringing up the rear, drop out and remain behind in the ballroom.* ZHIGALOV *and* DYMBA *come in and walk over to the table.*

BEST MAN (*shouts*). *Promenade! Messieurs, promenade!* (*Offstage.*) *Promenade!*

*The couples go out.*

YAT (*to* ZMEYUKINA). Have pity on me! Have a heart, enchanting Anna Martynovna!

ZMEYUKINA. Oh, for heaven's sake! I've told you already, I'm not in good voice today.

YAT. Please, I beg you, sing something, anything! Even just one note! Have pity on me! One note?

ZMEYUKINA. You're such a bore! (*Sits down and waves her fan.*)

YAT. Oh, you're absolutely heartless. To think that such a pitiless creature, if you'll pardon the expression, should possess such a wonderful, miraculous voice! With a voice like that, if you'll forgive my saying so, you shouldn't be getting involved in midwifery, no, you should be giving recitals in grand concert halls! For instance, the divine way you sing that little grace note – how does it go again? (*Sings.*) 'I loved thee once, but love is still in vain…' Wonderful!

ZMEYUKINA (*sings*). 'I loved thee once, and love might still perhaps…' Is that it?

YAT. That's it, exactly – wonderful!

ZMEYUKINA. No, my voice isn't up to it today. Here – wave this fan for me, it's so hot in here. (*To* APLOMBOV.) You're looking down in the dumps today, Mr Aplombov – what's the matter? That's no way for the groom to behave, now, is it. You should be ashamed of yourself. What's bothering you?

APLOMBOV. Marriage is a serious step, you know! You've got to consider it from all angles, every perspective.

ZMEYUKINA. Oh, you doubting Thomases really make me sick! You pollute the atmosphere with your presence so a person can hardly breathe! For heaven's sake, let me have some air! D'you hear? Give me some breathing space! (*Begins to sing.*)

YAT. Wonderful! Quite wonderful!

ZMEYUKINA. Keep that fan going – keep it going, I feel as if my heart's about to explode. Why is it so stuffy in here, tell me, please!

YAT. It's because you're sweating, dear lady, that's why.

ZMEYUKINA. Ugh! That's so vulgar! How dare you say that to me!

YAT. I'm terribly sorry. Of course, you're accustomed, so to speak, to high society, and...

ZMEYUKINA. Oh, leave me in peace! Just let me have poetry, ecstasy! Keep going, keep fanning!

ZHIGALOV (*to* DYMBA). Same again? (*Pours a drink.*) Yes, you can drink any time of day. The main thing, Dymba my friend, is not to forget the matter at hand. Drink, but keep your eye on the ball. And if it's about drinking, then why not have a drink, eh? You're permitted a drink, right? Your good health, sir!

*They drink.*

So, tell me, do you have tigers in Greece?

DYMBA. Yes.

ZHIGALOV. And lions?

DYMBA. Lions, yes. In Russia is nothing – in Greece is everything. There is father, uncles, brothers – here is nothing.

ZHIGALOV. Hm... D'you have whales in Greece?

DYMBA. Is everything, I tell you.

NASTASYA (*to* ZHIGALOV). Why is everybody drinking and picking at the food? It's time they were all sat down at the table. And stop prodding the lobster – that's to be kept for the General. He might still come.

ZHIGALOV. Do you have lobsters in Greece?

DYMBA. Yes… Is everything in Greece.

ZHIGALOV. What about civil servants? Got them in Greece?

NASTASYA. I can just imagine what the atmosphere's like in Greece!

ZHIGALOV. I dare say there's a lot of sharp practice. I mean, Greeks are pretty much like Armenians or gypsies. They'll sell you a sponge or a goldfish, and next thing they'll have the shirt off your back. A top-up?

NASTASYA. Never mind a top-up. It's time we were all at the table, it's getting on for midnight.

ZHIGALOV. We might as well sit down, then. (*Calls out.*) Ladies and gentlemen! If you don't mind, please! Supper time! Come on, you young people!

NASTASYA. Everybody, please. Come to the table!

ZMEYUKINA (*sitting down at the table*). Give me some poetry! 'But he, rebellious, seeks the storm / As if in storms lay peace…' Give me a storm!

YAT (*aside*). A wonderful woman! I'm in love – head over heels in love!

*Enter* DASHENKA, MOZGOVOY, BEST MAN, *other* GUESTS. *They take their places noisily at the table. A momentary pause; the offstage orchestra strikes up a march.*

MOZGOVOY (*stands up*). Ladies and gentlemen! I am obliged to inform you of the following; there are to be a great many toasts and speeches, so let's make a start without delay. Ladies and gentlemen, please raise your glasses to toast the newly-weds!

*The orchestra plays a fanfare; cheers, clinking of glasses.*

A kiss! A kiss!

ALL. A kiss!

APLOMBOV *and* DASHENKA *kiss*.

YAT. Marvellous! Absolutely marvellous! I am bound to say, ladies and gentlemen, with every justification, that this room, and indeed this entire establishment, are quite magnificent. First rate. Charming. But you know, there is one thing lacking, to make this triumphant occasion complete. Electric light, if you'll pardon the expression. Yes, electric lighting has been introduced in every country in the world, but Russia is still lagging behind.

ZHIGALOV (*pondering the matter*). Electricity... hm... Well, as I see it, electric light is just another swindle. They shove in a bit of live coal, and think you won't notice. No, my friend, if we're going to have light, don't give us a lump of coal, give us something substantial, something special, something you can get a hold of. Give us real light, you know what I mean? Natural, not artificial.

YAT. Listen, if you had a look inside an electric battery, what it's actually made of, you'd soon change your tune.

ZHIGALOV. I don't want to see one. It's all just a confidence trick, to make fools of people. Squeeze people dry, that's what they're up to, I know these types. And as for you, my dear young man, instead of defending charlatans, you should pour yourself a drink, and see to the others, while you're at it. And that's a fact!

APLOMBOV. I couldn't agree with you more, old man. What's the point of all this intellectual chit-chat? I've nothing against having a discussion about all manner of discoveries in the field of science, but, really, there's a time and place for everything. (*To* DASHENKA.) What do you think, *ma chère*?

DASHENKA. He just wants to show off how well educated he is, talking about stuff nobody understands.

NASTASYA. Well, thank God we've lived our whole lives with no education, and here we are marrying off a third daughter to a decent man. And if you think we're that ignorant, what are you doing here? Go away back to your clever friends!

YAT. Nastasya Timofeyevna, I've always respected your family, and if I've been going on about electric light, it's not to show off. I'll have a drink, yes, please. I've always wished a good husband for Dashenka, with all my heart. It's not easy these days, finding a decent man. People are all out for themselves, getting married for money.

APLOMBOV. Is that a hint?

YAT (*hastily*). I'm not hinting at anybody. Present company excepted. I'm just saying... in general... I do beg your pardon... I mean, everybody knows you two are in love. The dowry's a mere bagatelle.

NASTASYA. Bagatelle nothing! You're talking through your hat, sir. Apart from a thousand roubles in hard cash, we're giving them three ladies' coats, a bed, and all the furniture. Dowries like that don't grow on trees, you know!

YAT. I didn't mean to... I mean, the furniture, obviously – that's a very good thing, and the coats, well, of course... I'm just worried people might think I was hinting at something, and take offence.

NASTASYA. Well, don't hint. We invite you to this wedding out of respect for your mother and father, and you come out with remarks like that! If you knew Mr Aplombov here was marrying our daughter for money, why didn't you say so before this? (*Tearfully*.) I've nursed her, brought her up, cherished her – guarded her like a precious jewel, my darling baby girl...

APLOMBOV. You mean you actually believe him? Well, thanks a million – I'm most deeply grateful! (*To* YAT.) As for you, Mr Yat, friend of mine you may be, but I can't allow you to behave so outrageously in someone else's home. Kindly remove yourself from these premises!

YAT. What are you talking about?

APLOMBOV. I would like you to be as much of a gentleman as I am. In brief, sir, clear off!

*The orchestra strikes up a fanfare.*

GUESTS (*to* APLOMBOV). Leave him alone! That's enough! It's not worth it! Sit down! Leave him be!

YAT. I didn't mean... Honestly, I... I don't understand any of this... All right, all right, I'm leaving. But first pay me back the five roubles you borrowed from me last year to buy that embroidered waistcoat, if you don't mind my saying. I'll just have another drink, then I'll... er, then I'll be off. But first pay me what you owe me.

GUESTS. Oh, come on, that's enough! Stop, enough! It's not worth all the fuss!

BEST MAN (*shouts*). A toast, ladies and gentlemen! To the bride's mother and father – your good health!

*The orchestra strikes up a fanfare. Cheering.*

ZHIGALOV (*deeply moved, bows in all directions*). Thank you! Thank you, dear friends! I thank you from the bottom of my heart, that you haven't forgotten us, that you've all turned up, and haven't shunned us. And don't think for a minute that this is all some sort of confidence trick, some act I'm putting on. No, this is just how I feel – from the very depths of my soul! Nothing's too good for decent people – I thank you most humbly!

*He and* NASTASYA *exchange kisses.*

DASHENKA (*to her mother*). Mama, why are you crying? I'm so happy!

APLOMBOV. Your *maman* is upset at the thought of being separated from you. But I'd advise her to remember our recent conversation.

YAT. Don't cry, Nastasya Timofeyevna. I mean, you know what tears are, don't you. A psychological deficiency, that's all.

ZHIGALOV. So, do you have mushrooms in Greece?

DYMBA. Yes, yes. In Greece is everything.

ZHIGALOV. White ones? What about those big orangey ones?

DYMBA. Is white, is oranges, is everything in Greece.

MOZGOVOY. Kharlampy Spiridonych, it's your turn to make a speech! Ladies and gentlemen, let him speak!

GUESTS (*to* DYMBA). Speech! Speech! It's your turn!

DYMBA. What? What is? I not understand! What is, please?

ZMEYUKINA. No, no – don't you dare refuse, it's your turn. Come on, stand up!

DYMBA (*stands up, flustered*). I can say this… which is Russia, which is Greece. People which is in Russia now, which is in Greece… And people which sail in sea, in Russia they say sheep – no, sheeps… In other countries is all kinds railways… I understand good… We Greek, you Russian, and I not need nothing… I can say this… which is Greece, which is Russia…

*Enter* NYUNIN.

NYUNIN. Hold on, everybody – don't start eating yet! Wait, wait! Nastasya Timofeyevna, a minute, please – over here! (*Puffing and panting, takes* NASTASYA *aside*.) Listen… the General's just coming… I've found one at last… I'm absolutely worn out… A real General, solid, respectable, must be eighty at least, maybe even ninety…

NASTASYA. So when is he coming?

NYUNIN. Right this minute. You'll be grateful to me your whole life. This is the genuine article, an honest-to-God Napoleon! And he's not one of your foot soldiers, your cannon fodder, he's with the Fleet. Captain Second Grade by rank, that's equivalent to a Major-General, or a State Councillor in the civil service – absolutely the same. Higher, even!

NASTASYA. You're sure you're not having me on, Andryusha?

NYUNIN. Now, really, would I try and put one over on you? Just relax.

NASTASYA (*sighs*). I don't want to be wasting our money, Andryusha.

NYUNIN. Don't you worry, this is an absolute peach of a General! (*Raising his voice*.) So, anyway, I say to him: 'You've quite forgotten us, Your Excellency – that's not nice now, is it, Your Excellency – forgetting old friends, eh? Nastasya Timofeyevna,' I say, 'is a bit peeved.' (*Goes over to the table, and sits down*.) And then he says, 'Look here, my friend, how can I go if I don't know the groom?' 'Oh, come now, Your Excellency,' I say, 'Don't stand on ceremony. The groom's a fine young man, wears his heart on his sleeve,' I say, 'Works as a loan appraiser in a pawnshop, but don't think, Your Excellency,' I say, 'this is some sort of weedy penpusher, or a Jack the lad. No no – these days you'll even find respectable ladies working in pawnshops.' Anyway, he claps me on the shoulder, we smoke a Havana cigar, and he's on his way right now... Just wait, ladies and gentlemen, don't start eating...

APLOMBOV. So when is he arriving?

NYUNIN. Any minute now – he was putting on his galoshes when I left him. Ladies and gentlemen, wait, please – don't start eating.

APLOMBOV. Well, you'd better tell them to play a march.

NYUNIN (*shouts*). Hey, musicians! Let's have a march!

*The orchestra plays a march for a minute or so.*

WAITER (*announcing*). Mr Revunov-Karaulov!

ZHIGALOV, NASTASYA *and* NYUNIN *rush to greet* REVUNOV *as he enters.*

NASTASYA (*curtsying*). Your Excellency, so good of you to come!

REVUNOV. Delighted!

ZHIGALOV. We're simple people, Your Excellency, ordinary, honest folk – I hope you don't think we're up to something. Decent people come first with us, nothing's too good for them, so please, make yourself at home!

REVUNOV. Delighted!

NYUNIN. If I may do the introductions, Your Excellency… our newly-wed bridegroom Epaminond Maximovich Aplombov, with his newly-born… I mean his newly-wedded wife!… Ivan Mikhailych Yat, an employee of the telegraph service… A foreigner of Greek origin, pastry cook by profession, Kharlampy Spiridonich Dymba… Oh, and Osip Lukich Babelmandebsky! And so on and so forth – the rest aren't worth bothering about. Now, please do sit down, Your Excellency!

REVUNOV. Delighted! Excuse me, ladies and gentlemen, while I have a word with young Andryusha… (*Draws* NYUNIN *aside*.) I'm a little confused here, my dear fellow – why do you keep addressing me as Your Excellency? I'm not a General, you know. Captain Second Grade, that's even lower than Colonel.

NYUNIN (*speaks into his ear, as to a deaf person*). I know, I know, Fyodor Yakovlevich, but do me one favour, just let me call you Your Excellency. The family here's very old-fashioned, respect their elders and betters and all that, and they're impressed by rank…

REVUNOV. Well, if that's the way things are, of course… (*Goes back to the table*.) Delighted!

NASTASYA. Please sit down, Your Excellency! If you would be so kind… Do have something to eat, Your Excellency! Only you must excuse us – you're accustomed to all sorts of delicacies at home, of course, and we're just simple folk.

REVUNOV (*not hearing*). Eh? What's that you say? Hm… Yes, indeed… (*A pause*.) Oh, yes, people lived very simply and contentedly in the old days. I'm an officer, of course, but I still live a simple life. Young Andryusha there came to me today and invited me to this wedding. 'How can I go?' I said, 'I don't know anybody there. It'd be a bit awkward.' 'Not at all,' he says, 'They're simple folk, old-fashioned, they'll welcome any guest.' Well, if that's how it is, why not, eh? Delighted. Sitting alone at home's pretty boring, and if my presence at this wedding can bring somebody a bit of pleasure, then go ahead, do your duty, I say.

ZHIGALOV. So you're here out of the kindness of your heart, Your Excellency? I really respect that. I'm a simple man myself, no tricks, and I respect people like that. Now, eat up, Your Excellency!

APLOMBOV. So, have you been retired long, Your Excellency?

REVUNOV. Eh? Oh, yes, yes indeed. That's very true. Yes... Now, if you don't mind me saying so, this herring's quite sour... and the bread, the bread's bitter, you can't eat it...

ALL. A kiss! A kiss to sweeten it! A kiss! A kiss!

APLOMBOV *and* DASHENKA *kiss*.

REVUNOV. Hee-hee! Your good health! (*A pause.*) Yes, indeed... In the old days everything was simple, everybody was contented... Yes, I love simplicity... I'm quite old, you know, retired from the service in 1865... I'm seventy-two now... Yes. Of course, even in those days, people loved to put on a bit of a show... (*Notices* MOZGOVOY.) You wouldn't happen to be a sailor, young man?

MOZGOVOY. Yes, sir!

REVUNOV. Aha, yes! Yes indeed, it's always been a hard life, the Navy. Lots to think about, to rack your brains over. All sorts of little words, each, so to speak, with its own special meaning. For instance: 'Topmen aloft! Foresail and mainsail yards!' So what does that mean, eh? Your sailor understands, right? Hee-hee! Puts algebra to shame, doesn't it.

NYUNIN. A toast to His Excellency! To General Fyodor Yakovlevich Revunov-Karaulov – your good health, sir!

*The orchestra plays a fanfare. Cheers.*

YAT. His Excellency has been gracious enough to express himself on the difficulties of naval service. But is the telegraph service really any easier? No one can enter the telegraph service these days unless he is able to read and write in French and German. But for us, the hardest task is just sending a telegram. It's terribly difficult. If you'll permit me… listen… (*Taps out a Morse code message with a fork on the table.*)

REVUNOV. What does that mean?

YAT. That means: 'I respect you, Your Excellency, for your manifold virtues.' Now, was that easy, do you think? And what about this? (*Begins tapping.*)

REVUNOV. A bit louder, please – I can't hear.

YAT. That means: 'Madame, I'm so happy to be holding you in my arms.'

REVUNOV. Which madame are you referring to? Yes… (*To* MOZGOVOY.) Now, then – there's a stiff breeze blowing, and you've got to set the topgallants and royals. That's when you give the order: 'Topmen to the crosstrees, hoist topgallants and royals!' And while the sails are filling out on the yards, down on the deck they're hard at work, manning the halyards and braces…

BEST MAN (*gets to his feet*). Ladies and gentlemen…

REVUNOV (*interrupts*). Oh, yes, indeed – there are all sorts of commands. Yes… 'Hoist the foretopgallants and royals! Tighten the halyards!' Good, eh? But what does that mean exactly? It's very simple. They haul up the royal and topgallant sheets, you see? And raise the halyards at the same time, so as to square off the royal sheets and foresails as they're being raised, so when the sheets are finally pulled taut, and the halyards run up, the topgallants and royals are filled out and the yards are braced in relation to the direction of the wind…

NYUNIN. Fyodor Yakovlevich, our hostess is asking if you wouldn't mind changing the subject. People don't understand it, and they're getting bored.

REVUNOV. What? Who's bored? (*To* MOZGOVOY.) Young man! Just suppose your ship's lying to the wind under full sail on a starboard tack, and you have to bring her around to port – what command would you give? Eh? Well, I'll tell you. It's, 'Pipe all hands on deck, and wear to port!' Hee-hee!

NYUNIN. Fyodor Yakovlevich, that's enough – eat your supper.

REVUNOV. And as soon as everybody's up, you give the command: 'To your stations! Stand by to wear ship!' Oh, it's the life, I tell you. You give the command, then watch the sailors run to their stations like lightning, to spread the topgallants and stays. You can't help yourself, you just have to shout, 'Well done, my brave lads!' (*Starts coughing and spluttering.*)

BEST MAN (*hurriedly trying to take advantage of the hiatus*). On this day, as we are, so to speak, gathered to do honour to our beloved...

REVUNOV (*interrupts*). Oh, yes, sirs! And you've got to remember all that. For instance, there's, 'Foresail-sheets and mainsail-sheets, let fly!'

BEST MAN (*aggrieved*). Why does he keep interrupting? We won't have time for a single speech at this rate!

NASTASYA. We're simple peasant folk, Your Excellency. We don't understand any of this, and it'd be more use if you told us something about...

REVUNOV (*mishearing her*). No, thank you, I've already eaten. More goose, did you say? No, thanks. Oh, yes, I remember the old days – it's a fine life, eh, young man? Sailing along on the sea, not a care in the world, and... (*Moved, his voice trembling.*) Remember that feeling of joy when you have to tack. What sailor doesn't get all fired up, even just thinking of that manoeuvre? The minute you give the command: 'Pipe all hands on deck, prepare to tack!' It's as if an electric shock goes through everybody, from the captain down to the meanest matelot – everybody feels the same thrill.

ZMEYUKINA. This is so boring!

*General muttering.*

REVUNOV (*mishears*). No, no more, thank you – I've eaten already. (*Excited.*) So then everybody gets ready, all eyes on the first mate, as he gives the order: 'Haul the starboard foresail and mainsail stays, port crosstree stays and counterbraces on the port side!' It's all done in an instant. 'Let fly the foresheet and the jibsheet, hard a' starboard!' (*Gets to his feet.*) The ship rolls into the wind, and the sails start to fill out… 'On the stays, on the stays there, look lively!' His eyes are fixed on the main topsail, till that finally begins to flap in the wind, and then it's the last command: 'Loose the maintop bowline, pay out the stays!' And suddenly you're flying along, the timbers creaking – sheer pandemonium! It all goes off without a hitch, the tack's a success, we've brought her about!

NASTASYA (*flares up*). General, you're ruining everything! You ought to be ashamed of yourself, at your age.

REVUNOV (*mishears*). Porridge? No, I haven't had any – thank you.

NASTASYA (*loudly*). I'm saying you should be ashamed of yourself, at your age, General, you're spoiling everything!

NYUNIN (*embarrassed*). Ladies and gentlemen… I mean, really – is this worth it? Honestly!

REVUNOV. In the first place, I'm not a General, I'm a naval Captain, Second Grade, which equates in rank to an army Lieutenant-Colonel.

NASTASYA. Well, if you're not a General, why did you take our money? We didn't pay you all that money to be made fools of!

REVUNOV (*bewildered*). What money?

NASTASYA. You know perfectly well what money! You got your twenty-five roubles from Andrei Andreyevich…

(*To* NYUNIN.) And you, young man, should be ashamed of yourself. This isn't the sort of person I asked you to hire!

NYUNIN. Well, anyway – look, just forget it, it's not worth all this fuss.

REVUNOV. Hired? Paid? What the devil's going on?

APLOMBOV. If you'll allow me… I mean, you did receive twenty-five roubles from Andrei Andreyevich, didn't you?

REVUNOV. What twenty-five roubles? (*Understanding dawns.*) So that's what's going on? I see it all now. What a dirty trick – that's disgraceful!

APLOMBOV. But you did receive the money?

REVUNOV. I didn't receive any money. Get out of my sight! (*Stands up.*) What mean, despicable behaviour! To insult an old man, a sailor, an officer who's served his country… If this was respectable company, I'd challenge one of you to a duel, but what can I do in a place like this? (*Distraught.*) Where's the door? How do I get out of here? Waiter, show me the way out! Waiter! (*Makes to go.*) Despicable! Absolute dregs! (*Goes out.*)

NASTASYA. Andrei, what've you done with that twenty-five roubles?

NYUNIN. What's all the fuss about? Really, it's so trivial. Damn it, I don't know what you're talking about, but everybody's having a good time, right? (*Shouts.*) Ladies and gentlemen – to the bride and groom, a toast! Let's have some music! Music! A march!

*The orchestra strikes up a march.*

To the bride and groom!

ZMEYUKINA. I can't breathe! Let me have some air, you're suffocating me!

YAT (*in ecstasy*). Wonderful creature! Sublime!

*General murmur.*

BEST MAN (*straining to be heard*). Ladies and gentlemen!… On this, so to speak, auspicious…

*Curtain.*

# SWANSONG

*A dramatic study in one act*

**Characters**

VASILY VASILYICH SVETLOVIDOV, *a comedian, aged sixty-eight*

NIKITA IVANYCH, *the prompter, an old man*

*The action takes place on the stage of a middle-ranking provincial theatre, after the performance. To the right, a row of unpainted, rough-hewn doors lead off to the dressing rooms; to the left and rear, the empty stage is littered with odd props and rubbish, and in the centre is an overturned stool. It is night, and the theatre is in darkness.*

SVETLOVIDOV, *still in his stage costume as Calchas* [*in Euripides'* Iphigeneia in Aulis], *emerges from one of the dressing rooms, holding a candle.*

SVETLOVIDOV (*laughs*). Well, that's a joke. That's very funny. Fell asleep in the dressing room! Show finished ages ago, everybody's left the theatre, and there I am, out like a light, snoring my head off. Oh, you silly old goat. An old goat, sir – a silly old sod. Pissed as a newt again, nodded off in my chair. Yes, that was clever. Good for you, my darling. (*Shouts.*) Yegorka! Yegorka, damn it! Petrushka! They must've fallen asleep, the buggers – damn and blast them! Yegorka! (*Picks up the stool, sits on it, and stands the candle on the floor.*) Not a sound. My own echo, that's all the answer I'm getting. And to think I gave that pair a three-rouble note each today – now you won't see hide nor hair of them. They've legged it off home, most likely, and locked the theatre up. (*Twists his head round.*) Drunk! Ugh! My benefit show too, God only knows how much booze I've poured down my throat! My whole body stinks like a brewery, and my mouth's like the bottom of a parrot's cage, it's disgusting! (*A pause.*) What an idiot – the old fool's roaring drunk, and it's not even his birthday... ugh! God Almighty, my back's killing me, I've got a splitting headache, I'm shivering all over, and inside I feel like a cold, dark cellar. I mean, if I don't care for my health, I ought at least to act my age, damn buffoon that I am... (*A pause.*) Yes, old age. You can strut and fret all you like, but you're past it now. You can kiss goodbye to your sixty-eight years, they're

gone for ever. There's no turning back, you've drained the
bottle, there's nothing left but the dregs. Yes, indeed, the dregs.
Well, that's life, Vasily, old mate. Like it or not, it's time you
started rehearsing your role as a corpse, the Grim Reaper's just
round the corner. (*Peers out into the auditorium.*) You know,
I've been on the stage for forty-five years, and I think this is
the first time I've seen the theatre empty at night... Yes, the
first time... That's strange – damn it to hell, it's eerie!... (*Goes
up to the footlights.*) Can't see a thing... no, wait, I can just
make out the prompt booth... and there's a box, and a music
stand... the rest is pitch dark. A black bottomless pit, like the
grave itself, with Death lurking inside. Brrr! It's cold! And
there's a fierce draught from somewhere, like whistling down
a chimney – a genuine honest-to-God haunted house! Damn it,
this place is giving me the creeps – I've got shivers up and
down my spine. (*Shouts.*) Yegorka! Petrushka! Where the
devil are you? Oh, Lord, why did I have to mention the devil?
Just put all these things out of your mind – horrible words.
And give up the drink. You're an old man, for God's sake, it's
time you were dead... at sixty-eight, decent people get up
early, they go to church, they're preparing themselves for
death, but you... oh, dear God! Swearing like a trooper, blind
drunk, in this idiotic get-up, what do you look like? I'd better
get changed right now. Horrible! I mean, sitting here the
whole night, you could die of sheer fright... (*Makes to exit to
his dressing room.*)

*At that moment,* NIKITA IVANYCH, *wearing a white
dressing gown, emerges from a far dressing room at the rear
of the stage.* SVETLOVIDOV *catches sight of him, lets out a
terrified shriek and staggers back.*

SVETLOVIDOV. Who's that? What do you want? Who do you
want? (*Stamps his foot.*) Who are you?

NIKITA IVANYCH. It's only me, sir!

SVETLOVIDOV. Who's me?

NIKITA IVANYCH (*moves slowly towards him*). It's me, sir –
Nikita Ivanych, the prompter. Vasil Vasilich, it's only me!

SVETLOVIDOV (*slumps down onto the stool, breathing heavily and trembling all over*). Oh, my God! Who is it? Is it you... Nikita, is it? What are you doing here?

NIKITA IVANYCH. I sleep in the dressing rooms here at night, sir. Only please don't tell the manager, sir... I've nowhere else to go, sir, honest to God I haven't.

SVETLOVIDOV. So it's you, Nikita... Good God Almighty! You know I took sixteen curtain calls, three bouquets, they gave me all sorts of other things... they were absolutely ecstatic, yet not one single soul could be bothered to wake up an old drunk man in his dressing room and take him home! I'm an old man, Nikita – sixty-eight years of age... And ill! I'm weak – I haven't the spirit for this any longer... (*Falls into the prompter's arms and weeps.*) Don't leave me, Nikita, I'm old and helpless, it's time I was dead. I'm frightened, terribly frightened!

NIKITA IVANYCH (*tenderly and respectfully*). Vasil Vasilich, it's time you went home, sir.

SVETLOVIDOV. I can't! I haven't got a home – no, no, no!

NIKITA IVANYCH. Oh, Lord, sir – you haven't forgotten where you live?

SVETLOVIDOV. I'm not going to that place, I don't want to! I'm all alone there... I've got nobody, Nikita, no family, no wife, no children. I'm all alone, like the wind blowing over the fields. I'm going to die, and nobody'll remember me. It's a terrible thing, to be alone... nobody to comfort me, nobody to give me a hug, nobody to put me to bed when I'm drunk. Who do I belong to? Who needs me? Who loves me? Nobody loves me, Nikita!

NIKITA IVANYCH (*in tears*). Your audience loves you, Vasil Vasilich!

SVETLOVIDOV. My audience has gone home, they're sound asleep now, they've forgotten their old clown. No, nobody needs me, nobody loves me. I've no wife, no children...

NIKITA IVANYCH. So? Don't upset yourself...

SVETLOVIDOV. I mean, I'm a human being, I'm alive – that's warm blood coursing through my veins, not water. And I'm a gentleman, Nikita, a member of the nobility. Before I landed in this pit I served in the army, in the artillery. A fine young man I was too, handsome, high-minded, brave, keen as mustard! My God, whatever happened to all that? Well, then I became an actor – and what an actor, Nikita, eh? (*Lifts himself up, leaning on the prompter's arm.*) Yes, what happened to all that, where have they gone, the snows of yesteryear, eh? I've just looked down into that pit now, and I remember it all, everything! That same pit, Nikita, that abyss has swallowed up forty-five years of my life, and what a life it's been! I look into it now, and I see it all, down to the last detail, as clearly as I can see your face. The joys of youth, faith, passion, the love of women! Women, Nikita!

NIKITA IVANYCH. Vasil Vasilich, sir – it's time you were in bed.

SVETLOVIDOV. When I was a young actor, in the first stirrings of that passion, there was a young woman who fell in love with me for my acting. She was exquisite, slender as a young poplar, innocent and pure, radiant as a summer dawn! The darkest night was powerless to resist her blue eyes, the miracle of her smile. Ocean waves crash against rocks, but against the waves of her hair cliffs, icebergs, even snow-capped mountains hurled themselves in vain! I remember standing before her once, as I'm standing before you now. At that moment, I'd never seen her so beautiful, and she looked at me in such a way... I'll never forget that look, not even in my grave. Such softness, like velvet, such depth of feeling, all the sparkle of youth! I was intoxicated, ecstatic – I fell to my knees, and begged her to make my happiness complete... (*Audibly pained.*) But she... she said, 'Give up the stage!' *Give up the stage!* Do you understand? She could love an actor, but to become an actor's wife? Never! I remember I was on stage that day... some vulgar clown's part, and while I was out there hamming it up, I felt the scales falling from my eyes. It was then I realised there was no such thing as a sacred art – it was all delusion and trickery, and I was a mere slave, a plaything of other people's idle fancy – a buffoon, a court jester! Yes, I'd got the measure of my audience. Since then, I've put no trust in their applause, their bouquets, their enthusiasm. Oh, yes, Nikita, they applaud me, they'll pay a rouble for my photograph, but I'm a stranger to them. I'm something they've picked up on their shoe, an old whore, near as damn it! Oh, they'll condescend to make my acquaintance – it flatters their vanity – but God forbid I should marry their sister or their daughter. No, I don't trust them! (*Slumps down on the stool.*) I've no faith in them!

NIKITA IVANYCH. Vasil Vasilich, you don't look well! You've even got me frightened... For mercy's sake, sir, let's take you home.

SVETLOVIDOV. That's when I had my eyes opened, Nikita, and paid dearly for the privilege. After that affair... after that girl... well, I started to drift, aimlessly, living from day to day, taking no thought for the morrow. I played all manner of clowns and grinning buffoons, while my brains turned to mush. Oh yes, I was a true artist once, genuinely talented, but I frittered my talent away, buried it completely, coarsened my voice and delivery, lost my looks – let myself go, yes. And it's devoured me, that damned bottomless pit, it's swallowed me up! I've never felt like this before, but tonight... when I woke up, I looked back, and there behind me lay all my sixty-eight years. I've seen old age now, and it's all over – *finita la commedia*! The song is ended! (*Breaks down, sobs.*) It's ended!

NIKITA IVANYCH. Vasil Vasilich, don't – please don't! Oh, Lord! Don't upset yourself, sir, please! (*Shouts.*) Petrushka! Yegorka!

SVETLOVIDOV. And I had real talent, you know, and such power! You can't imagine how eloquent I was, how graceful – the range of emotions I could convey, how many strings I could play on, in this breast of mine! (*Pounds his chest.*)

It makes me choke, even to think of it. Listen – listen, old man – once I've got my breath back... This is from *Borís Godunov*... (*Declaims part of the Pretender's speech, Scene XIII.*)

> '...The shade of Tsar Iván
> Made me his son; his dread voice from the tomb
> Named me Dimítri, which stirred up the people
> To my cause, and ensured Borís's doom.
> I am Tsarévich. Now, enough! What shame
> That I should kneel before a Polish maid...'

Not bad, eh? Wait now, this is from *King Lear*. The sky's pitch black, and it's pouring rain, right? There's a thunderstorm – roarrrr! And lightning – fizzzz! It streaks across the whole sky, and then... Listen. (*Declaims from* King Lear, *Act III, Scene II.*)

> 'Blow, winds, and crack your cheeks! Rage! Blow!
> You cataracts and hurricanoes, spout
> Till you have drench'd our steeples, drown'd the cocks!
> You sulphurous, thought-executing fires,
> Vaunt-couriers of oak-cleaving thunderbolts,
> Singe my white head! And thou, all-shaking thunder,
> Strike flat the thick rotundity o' the world!
> Crack nature's moulds, all germens spill at once,
> That make ingrateful man!...'

(*Impatiently.*) Well, come on, come on – the Fool! Your cue – give me the Fool's line – I can't wait!

NIKITA IVANYCH (*speaks the Fool's part*). 'O, nuncle, court holy-water in a dry house is better than this rain-water out o' door. Good nuncle, in, and ask thy daughters' blessing. Here's a night pities neither wise men nor fools...'

SVETLOVIDOV.
> 'Rumble thy bellyful! Spit, fire! Spout, rain!
> Nor rain, wind, thunder, fire, are my daughters:
> I tax not you, you elements, with unkindness:
> I never gave you kingdom, call'd you children...'

Ah, now there's power, talent, artistry! Let's try something else – something of the same kind – harking back to the good old days. Let me think... (*Laughs delightedly.*) Something from *Hamlet*. Right, I'll begin... Now, how does it go again? Ah, I've got it... (*Declaims from* Hamlet, *Act III, Scene II*.)

'O, the recorder, let me see! To withdraw with you. Why do you go about to recover the wind of me, as if you would drive me into a toil?'

NIKITA IVANYCH. 'O, my lord, if my duty be too bold, my love is too unmannerly.'

SVETLOVIDOV. 'I do not well understand that. Will you play upon this pipe?'

NIKITA IVANYCH. 'My lord, I cannot.'

SVETLOVIDOV. 'I pray you.'

NIKITA IVANYCH. 'Believe me, I cannot.'

SVETLOVIDOV. 'I do beseech you.'

NIKITA IVANYCH. 'I know no touch of it, my lord.'

SVETLOVIDOV. ''Tis as easy as lying: govern these ventages with your finger and thumb, give it breath with your mouth, and it will discourse most eloquent music. Look you, these are the stops.'

NIKITA IVANYCH. 'But these cannot I command to any utterance of harmony; I have not the skill.'

SVETLOVIDOV. 'Why, look you now, how unworthy a thing you make of me! You would play upon me; you would seem to know my stops; you would pluck out the heart of my mystery; you would sound me from my lowest note to the top of my compass: and there is much music, excellent voice in this little organ, yet cannot you make it speak. 'Sblood, do you think I am easier to be played on than a pipe? Call me what instrument you will, though you can fret me, you cannot play upon me!'

(*Laughs and claps his hands.*) Bravo! Encore! Bravo! Where the hell's old age now, eh? There's no such thing as old age, it's all rubbish, sheer nonsense! I can feel the energy pulsing though every vein, like a fountain – this is youth, freshness, the very stuff of life! Where there's genius, Nikita, there's no room for old age! You think I'm mad, Nikita? I've gone off my head? Hold on, just let me pull myself together... Oh, dear God! Now, listen to this – the tenderness, and subtlety, the music of it... Ssshh! Quiet... (*Declaims from Pushkin's* Poltava, *Canto II.*)

> 'A silent, moonlit night in the Ukraine;
> The sky is clear, the stars are points of light.
> The drowsy air hangs listless on the plain,
> And barely stirs the poplars silvery-white...'

*A door is heard opening.*

What was that?

NIKITA IVANYCH. That must be Petrushka and Yegorka coming back, sir. Yes, that's real talent, Vasil Vasilich — that's genius!

SVETLOVIDOV (*calls out, turning in the direction of the noise*). Come up here, my bold lads! (*To* NIKITA IVANYCH.) Let's go and get dressed. No, there's no such thing as old age, it's all stuff and nonsense. (*Laughs heartily.*) What are you crying about? My fine old fool, why all the tears? That's not good, you know! That really isn't good! Come on, come on, that's enough, old man, stop looking at me like that! What are you staring at? Come on, come on! (*Tearfully embraces him.*) There's no need for tears. Where there's art, where there's genius, there's no place for old age, no place for loneliness, no place for sickness – and death itself is half... (*Weeps.*) No, Nikita, we've sung our song. What sort of genius am I? A squeezed lemon, a melted icicle, a rusty old nail. And you? An old theatre rat, a prompter... Come on, let's go.

*They make to go out.*

And I'm no genius. When it comes to serious drama, I'm only fit for a walk-on in Fortinbras's retinue. And I'm too old even for that... Yes... You remember that bit in *Othello*, Nikita? (*Declaims from* Othello, *Act III, Scene III.*)

> 'Farewell the tranquil mind! Farewell content!
> Farewell the plumèd troops, and the big wars,
> That makes ambition virtue! O, farewell!
> Farewell the neighing steed, and the shrill trump,
> The spirit-stirring drum, the ear-piercing fife,
> The royal banner, and all quality,
> Pride, pomp, and circumstance of glorious war!...'

NIKITA IVANYCH. Genius, sheer genius!

SVETLOVIDOV. Or what about this? (*Declaims from Chatsky's final speech in Griboyedov's* Woe from Wit, *Act IV, Scene XIV.*)

> 'Away, away from Moscow, never to return!
> Ride off, without a backward glance, without remorse,
> To seek some refuge from this world's unfeeling scorn –
> Some solace for the wounded heart... To horse! To horse!'

SVETLOVIDOV *and* NIKITA IVANYCH *go out*.

*The curtain is slowly lowered.*

# ON THE EVILS OF TOBACCO

*A dramatic monologue in one act*

## Characters

IVAN IVANOVICH NYUKHIN, *husband of his wife, the proprietress of a music and boarding school for young ladies*

*The scene represents the platform stage of a small-town social club.*

NYUKHIN, *with long side whiskers, no moustache, and dressed in a rusty old frock coat, makes a grand entrance, bows, and straightens his waistcoat.*

NYUKHIN. Nyukhin... Ivan Ivanovich Nyukhin... Gracious ladies, and in a manner of speaking, gracious gentlemen also... (*Runs his fingers through his side whiskers.*) The suggestion has been put to my good wife that I should give a lecture at this point, for charity, on some sort of popular subject. Well, why not? Why not a lecture, eh? I mean, it's all the same to me. Of course, I'm not a professor, university degrees aren't my forte, but nonetheless and even so, for the past thirty years, without a break, unstinting – to the detriment, one might even say, of my health and well-being and suchlike – I have laboured over questions of a rigorously scientific nature, pondered them at length, and on occasion even written, believe it or not, scholarly articles – well, not exactly scholarly, let's say, but if you'll pardon the expression – sort of scholarly. Among other things, I recently penned an enormous article entitled 'On the Harm Caused by Certain Insects'. My daughters enjoyed it hugely, especially the section on bedbugs. I read it aloud to them, then tore it up. After all, it doesn't matter what you write, you'll still need insecticide to get rid of them. We've even got them in the piano.

Anyway, the subject I have, so to speak, chosen for my lecture today is the harm done to mankind by the use of tobacco. I do actually smoke myself, but my wife ordered me to talk about the harm caused by tobacco, so there was no point in further conversation. Well, then – tobacco, why not, eh? It's all the same to me, but for you, gracious ladies and gentlemen, I suggest you give this lecture of mine the serious attention it deserves, else who knows what might happen. Anyone who is alarmed at the thought of a dry scientific lecture, anyone who doesn't fancy the idea, well, they don't need to listen, they can leave now. (*Adjusts his waistcoat.*) In particular, I would recommend the attention of any members of the medical profession here today, who will find a great deal of useful information in my lecture, insofar as tobacco, aside from its injurious effects, is also employed in medicine. For example, if you place a fly in a snuffbox, it will die, probably from a nervous breakdown. First and foremost, though, tobacco is a plant...

Actually, when I'm giving a lecture, my right eye tends to start twitching, but don't take any notice of that, it's just nerves. I'm an extremely nervous person, as a general rule, and my eye first began twitching in 1889, on the thirteenth of September, the same day as my wife gave birth, in a manner of speaking, to our fourth daughter, Varvara. All my daughters were born on the thirteenth. However... (*Glances at his pocket watch.*) bearing in mind the shortage of time, we'd better not stray too far from the subject of our lecture. I should point out, though, that my wife runs a music school and private boarding school... well, not exactly a boarding school, but something along those lines. Just between ourselves, my wife likes to complain about being short of things, but she has a fair sum tucked away, forty or fifty thousand, while I haven't a bean, not a single kopeck to my name. Anyway, there's no point in going on about it. At the boarding school, I'm in charge of the housekeeping department. I purchase all the provisions, keep an eye on the hired help, write up the accounts, bind the students' notebooks, get rid of the bedbugs, take my wife's little dog for walks, and trap the mice...

One of my duties yesterday evening was to dole out the flour and butter for the cook, since we were planning to have pancakes. Well, to cut a long story short, this morning, after the pancakes had already been made, my wife came into the kitchen to announce that three of the students wouldn't be having any pancakes, because they had swollen glands. So, as it turned out, we'd baked a few surplus pancakes. Well, then, what do you suggest we do with them? At first my wife told me to take them down to the cellar, but after some thought, and a bit more thought, she said: 'Oh, just eat them yourself, you miserable old scarecrow!' That's what she calls me when she's in a bad mood: scarecrow, or snake-in-the-grass, or Satan, even. I mean, really, do I look like Satan? She's always in a bad mood. So I didn't just eat those pancakes, I actually gulped them down without chewing, because I'm constantly hungry. Yesterday, for instance, she didn't give me any dinner. 'You're an old scarecrow,' she said, 'It's a waste of time feeding you.'

Well, anyway… (*Looks at his pocket watch.*) we've been rambling on a bit, drifted away from our subject. Let us continue. Although I'm sure you'd much rather be listening to a love song, or a symphony of some kind, or an aria… (*Sings.*) 'In the heat of battle, we shall not blink an eye…' Now, what's that out of? I can't remember. Incidentally, I forgot to tell you, in my wife's music school, apart from attending to the housekeeping, I'm also responsible for the teaching of mathematics, physics, chemistry, geography, history, tonic sol-fa, literature, and so on. My wife charges an additional fee for dance, singing, and drawing lessons, although I teach dance and singing as well. Our musical establishment is situated at No. 13, Five Dogs Lane. That's probably why I've had so much bad luck in my life, the fact that we live at No. 13. And my daughters were all born on the thirteenth, and our house has thirteen windows…

Well, there's no point in going on about it. If you want to discuss these things further, my wife can be found at home any time of the day, and if you'd like a prospectus of the school, they're on sale from the doorman at thirty kopecks. (*Pulls a few copies from his pocket.*) Actually, you can get them from me, if you like. Now, thirty kopecks – who'd like one? (*A pause.*) Nobody? All right, then – twenty kopecks! (*A pause.*) That's a pity. Yes, No. 13! I've never had any luck, failed at everything. I've grown old – old and stupid… Here I am giving a lecture, I look happy enough, but what I'd really like to do is shriek at the top of my lungs, or take flight to the back of beyond somewhere. And there isn't anybody I can complain to, I just feel like crying... 'But what about your daughters?' you'll say. What daughters? I try to speak to them, all they do is laugh... My wife has seven daughters... No, I tell a lie, it's six, I think... (*Brightly.*) Seven! Anna, she's the eldest, she's twenty-seven, the youngest is seventeen. Gracious ladies and gentlemen! (*Looks around.*) I'm thoroughly miserable, I've become a fool, a nonentity, but in point of fact, what you see before you is the luckiest father alive. And essentially that's just as it should be, I wouldn't dare say otherwise. Oh, if only you knew! I've lived with my wife now for thirty-three years, and I can truthfully say these have been the best years of my life – well, maybe not the best, but generally speaking... To cut a long story short, they've flown past, in one happy instant, and frankly, to hell with the lot of them. (*Looks around.*) Anyway, I don't think she's arrived yet, she's not here, and I can say whatever I like... I'm scared stiff, you know, terrified whenever she looks at me. Yes, so as I was saying, my daughters aren't married yet, and time's passing. It's probably because they're shy, and because men never get to see them. My wife won't have soirées at home, she never invites anybody to dinner, she's an extremely mean, bad-tempered, sour-faced woman, and that's why nobody ever comes near us, but... but... I'll let you in on a secret... (*Comes forward to the edge of the platform.*) My wife's daughters can be viewed on high days and holidays at their aunt's, Natalya Semyonovna, that is – the one who suffers from rheumatism and goes about in a sort of yellow frock with black spots, that make it look as if she was covered in cockroaches. You'll even get offered a bite to eat at her place. And when my wife isn't there, you can also... (*Mimes taking a drink.*) I should mention that I get drunk after just one glass, and that makes me feel really good, and at the same time terribly sad, I can't tell you how sad. For some reason or other I start thinking about when I was young, and I don't know why, but I just want to run away – oh, if you only knew how much I want that! (*Excitedly.*) Yes, run away! Just dump everything and run, without so much as a backward glance... but where to? Who cares where to? Just

run away from this cheap, nasty, vulgar life, this life that's
turned me into a pathetic old fool, a pathetic old halfwit –
run away from this stupid, petty, evil, evil, evil miser of a
woman – this wife who has tormented me for thirty-three
years; run away from the music, from the kitchen, from my
wife's money, from all these trivialities and banalities, and
come to a stop in some far-off, distant field, and just stand
there like a tree, or a fencepost, or a scarecrow, yes, under
the wide, open sky – stand there the whole night, gazing up
at the shining, silent moon, and just forget... forget...

Oh, how I wish I could remember nothing! How I'd love to
tear off this wretched old frock coat, the one I got married in,
thirty years ago... (*Rips off his coat.*) The one I'm still
constantly giving lectures in, for charity... There! (*Throws
his coat on the floor and stamps on it.*) There! I'm old, I'm
poor, I'm as pathetic as this shabby old waistcoat – see, the
back of it's coming apart at the seams... (*Takes it off to
display it.*) I don't need anything! I'm above all this, I'm
better than this, I was young once, and clever, I studied at the
university, I had dreams, I thought of myself as a human
being... Now I don't need anything! Nothing but peace,
that's all... just peace. (*Glances off to the side, hurriedly puts
on his waistcoat again.*) However, my wife's backstage...
She's here, and she's waiting for me. (*Looks at his pocket
watch.*) My time's up... If she asks, then please tell her... if
you'd be so kind... tell her that the lecture was... that the
scarecrow, that is to say, me, conducted himself with
dignity... (*Looks off to the side, clears his throat.*) She's
looking this way... (*Raises his voice.*) So, following on from
the proposition that tobacco contains within itself a virulent
poison, which I've just been describing, smoking should be
avoided at all costs, and I shall allow myself to hope, in a
manner of speaking, that this lecture of mine on 'The Evils
of Tobacco' will be of some benefit. Now, I've said my
piece. *Dixi et animam levavi...* (*Bows, and makes a grand
exit.*)

*Curtain.*

**Other Chekhov titles published by Nick Hern Books**

Chekhov: Four Plays
*translated by Stephen Mulrine*

The Cherry Orchard
*translated by Stephen Mulrine*

Ivanov
*translated by Stephen Mulrine*

Seagull
*translated by Charlotte Pyke, John Kerr
and Joseph Blatchley*

The Seagull
*translated by Stephen Mulrine*

Three Sisters
*translated by Stephen Mulrine*

Three Sisters
*translated by Nicholas Wright*

Uncle Vanya
*translated by Stephen Mulrine*

**A unique collection of everything that Chekhov wrote about the theatre.**

Chekhov started writing about theatre in newspaper articles and in his own letters even before he began writing plays. Later, he wrote in detail about his own plays to his lifelong friend and mentor Alexei Suvorin, his wife and leading actress, Olga Knipper, and to the two directors of the Moscow Art Theatre, Stanislavsky and Nemirovich-Danchenko.

Collected for this volume, these writings reveal Chekhov's instinctive curiosity about the way theatre works – and his concerns about how best to realise his own intentions as a playwright. Often peppery, passionate, even distraught, as he feels his plays misinterpreted or undermined, Chekhov comes over in these pages as a true man of the theatre.

'This book builds a strong picture of theatrical life in Moscow and St Petersburg just before and at the turn of the last century… It can also serve as a tangential autobiography since, through its pages, it is possible to learn much about its subject's life and work' *British Theatre Guide*

**www.nickhernbooks.co.uk**

facebook.com/nickhernbooks

twitter.com/nickhernbooks